Better Homes and Gardens®

Additions

YOUR GUIDE TO PLANNING AND REMODELING

Better Homes and Gardens® Books
Des Moines, Iowa

Better Homes and Gardens® Books
An imprint of Meredith® Books

Additions: Your Guide to Planning and Remodeling
Project Editor: Steve Cooper
Contributing Editor: John Riha
Associate Art Director: Lynda Haupert
Contributing Designer: Michael Burns
Copy Chief: Angela K. Renkoski
Electronic Production Coordinator: Paula Forest
Editorial Assistant: Susan McBroom
Art Assistant: Jennifer Norris
Production Manager: Douglas Johnston
Prepress Coordinator: Marjorie J. Schenkelberg

Meredith® Books
Editor in Chief: James D. Blume
Managing Editor: Greg Kayko
Executive Shelter Editor: Denise L. Caringer
Vice President, General Manager: Jamie L. Martin

***Better Homes and Gardens®* Magazine**
Editor in Chief: Jean LemMon
Executive Building Editor: Joan McCloskey

Meredith Publishing Group
President, Publishing Group: Christopher Little
Vice President and Publishing Director: John P. Loughlin

Meredith Corporation
Chairman of the Board: Jack D. Rehm
Chief Executive Officer: William T. Kerr
Chairman of the Executive Committee: E. T. Meredith III

Cover photograph: This addition is shown on pages 100 and 101.

All of us at Better Homes and Gardens® Books are dedicated to providing you with information and ideas you need to enhance your home. We welcome your comments and suggestions about this book on additions. Write to us at: Better Homes and Gardens® Books, Do-It-Yourself Editorial Department, RW–206, 1716 Locust St., Des Moines, IA 50309–3023.

Contents

About this book

We've planned this book in five broad phases designed to help guide you through a successful project, whatever the size, age, or style of your home. At this point, you may have a good idea of the kind of extra space you need—or you may only know that your present home feels cramped or closed in. Wherever you are in the dreaming process, this book will help you look at, then narrow, your options and arrive at a plan that will add comfort, function, and style to your home.

You will learn how to evaluate your home's systems and floor plan, make design choices, and work with design and building professionals. Along the way, we'll give you practical exercises intended to help you understand your needs, your dreams, and all the possibilities that your home offers.

Examine Your Options

A well-planned addition can give your home newfound space, livability, comfort—and great style.

There are many excellent reasons why you would create additional space for your home. Your kitchen might be small and dark and need to be opened up with fresh colors and plenty of light. It may be that your growing family requires another bedroom or bathroom. Or perhaps you envision a new family room with a wall of windows that takes advantage of a lovely garden vista. Whatever your needs, an addition may provide the solution. As you work through your planning phases, it is important to determine the scope of your project and select options that are in keeping with your budget. For example, you can "add" space simply by removing a wall between two rooms. A small bumped-out bay or window seat may be all you need to turn a cramped room into an expansive and airy one.

Before you remodel, take a deep breath. Adding on can be a big job. It can disrupt your life, devour your time, put pressure on your finances, and strain family relationships. Additions also bring with them a sometimes complicated snarl of decisions—and a surprising amount of dust and mess. But the process can be exciting and satisfying, too. Adding on gives you the chance to make your home "live" and look the way *you* want it to. And, instead of moving, building an addition means you won't have to give up your mature landscaping, the kids' best friends and good schools, and your treasured neighbors.

Look forward to the finished project. Whatever your reason for adding on, you will find the process filled with hard work, yes, but also with great rewards—especially when it's time to show off your remodeled home to family and friends.

◀ *Bright, sunny mornings invite us to create additions that reach out and embrace the view. Before this charming, light-filled sitting room was built, the rear of this home offered only a few small windows through which to glimpse the garden and out-of-doors.*

▲ *Love your yard and views of trees and flowers? The owners of this home did, so they added this comfortably sunny room to take advantage of their home's setting. It's part of a strong trend as remodeling dollars are invested in rooms that connect to nature.*

Basic Room Additions

Before tackling detailed planning, you'll want to consider what's possible with an addition. As a starting place, let's examine the six basic design options you have.

▼ Outside structures

Among the most popular additions, porches and sunrooms form inviting connections between a home and its outdoor spaces. Whether open, screened, or glassed-in, such rooms extend our living spaces and provide a place for retreating or for relaxed entertaining.

▲ Bump-outs

These small-scale additions are created by extending a wall only a few feet. The space gain itself may be small, but the effect is great. Imagine, for example, how a bumped-out dining bay or window seat can loosen up a tight room and transform a once-flat wall into a welcome architectural asset.

➤ Room additions

Many contractors offer package deals on standard-size room additions. Sometimes an addition will house a single room—that coveted new master suite you've always wanted or an inviting new family room.

▼ Second-story additions

If you have big dreams but a small or narrow lot, you may have no way to go but up. This strategy calls for consulting with an architect and/or an engineer about how much load your existing walls and foundation can handle. Also, be sure to ask local officials whether there are any height restrictions in your area.

▼ Wing additions

When you need something more than a single-room addition, you may add an entire wing. This was common in the 1800s as families grew and prospered. With today's smaller building lots, wing additions are less common, because they often result in a house that is too big for its site and neighborhood, and, therefore, tough to resell. Look at your situation carefully before choosing this option.

▼ Two-story additions

These additions are rare, but they can provide a creative solution to tough problems. You can attach a tower directly to the house or build a two-story addition away from the main house and connect the two structures with passageways on each level.

Assess Your Home's Systems

▲ *New electrical service was a must when this modern bedroom suite was built onto the end of a 42-year-old home in Memphis, Tennessee.*

As you inspect the structure of your house, you will also look closely at its systems. You need to know that everything is working properly and will continue to meet the demands of your growing house. A qualified building inspector will be able to evaluate the condition of your existing plumbing, electrical, and heating, ventilating, and cooling (HVAC) systems, and should be able to offer advice about the requirements of your addition. A remodeling contractor or qualified subcontractor will be able to give you detailed answers about the work involved and the costs of repairing or extending your systems.

Start with water. Examine the condition of your home's water lines and drain pipes. Look for signs of corrosion, rust, or leaks. If you are adding new pipes, determine what type of piping is already in place so you can match the old and new parts of the system. Your home inspector should be able to identify any lead piping. This should be replaced so your family won't be exposed to toxic metal leaching into the water.

Safety First

Inspection exposes you to dangers, so proceed cautiously and watch out for the following hazards. If in doubt, let the pros do the work.

Asbestos. Older flooring tiles, ceiling tiles, and insulation may contain asbestos—a mineral fiber that becomes highly carcinogenic when inhaled. Materials containing this substance are best left undisturbed. They can be covered by new materials, but should not be cut, ripped, or sanded, if at all possible. Evaluating the presence of asbestos and how to deal with it is a job for professionals.

Lead. Lead can cause brain damage and disease, particularly in children and the elderly.

Do-it-yourself test kits and lead-abatement services can tell you if the paint in your home contains lead—and what to do about it. If your home was built before 1978, the year lead was banned from paint production, chances are that the lead test will be positive. The worst thing you can do is sand old lead paint, because that sends the tiny granules airborne and you breathe them in. The dust that stays behind also poses risk.

Molds. As you remodel, you will be exposing yourself to various molds in your house. Since construction is dirty work that unavoidably stirs up many microorganisms, wear a face mask to limit exposure and protect your lungs.

▲ *Where's the addition? New construction blends so smoothly with the old that few would guess the gable with the round window was added on.*

Although they have been banned from use, lead water pipes were commonly installed in homes built through the 1960s. Many other homes have galvanized iron pipes. This type of piping often becomes caked with sediment during years of use and may need to be replaced if the buildup restricts water flow.

Examine your water heater, too. If you plan to expand your water system, you'll want to determine whether your current water heater can handle a heavier load. In homes where a bathroom is being added quite a distance from the water heater, consider installing a European-style instant water heater. These units fit into the wall of your bathroom and heat water on demand. Those who live with a septic system will have to look at the impact of the addition. Will it alter or restrict your drainage field in any way? Can your septic system handle the increased demands of another bathroom or water-using appliance?

How's the electrical system? Find out if your system can handle modern electrical loads. It should have at least 100-ampere, 240-volt, three-wire service. It also needs modern circuit breakers or fuses. Be aware that many homes of the 1970s were built with potentially dangerous aluminum wiring, which can slip out of junction boxes and create shorts. If you have this type of wiring, change it completely or upgrade your system with special connectors and junction boxes that won't allow it to slip.

Check the HVAC. An addition will tax your existing furnace and air-conditioner. An expert can tell you if your system is up to the job. If changes must be made, this is a great time to upgrade to newer, high-efficiency units. Also, consider installing whole-house air cleaning and ventilating systems, and ask your heating-and-cooling professional about electronic air cleaners or high-efficiency, whole-house media filters.

Layout Logic

Planning an addition gives you the chance to add space and, at the same time, to improve your home's layout. You probably have a good idea where traffic patterns work in your home and where they don't—areas where everything flows sensibly from room to room, and those places where people seem to get hung up in a snarl of doors and doorways. As you plan your addition, you might have the opportunity to redesign some of your home's problem areas so that they work better. Can you open up that cramped passageway between the dining room and kitchen? Is your new breakfast room situated where it can soak up morning sunlight, the way you always dreamed it would?

To understand your present floor plan's strengths and weaknesses, draw a simple diagram of the layout. This doesn't have to look professional—it's just a study tool that will help you identify problem areas. You will be creating a more detailed floor plan later.

▲ *The owners replaced an awkward passageway with this sunny, inviting nook. See plan, below.*

▼ *This well-planned addition and remodeling created the nook, mudroom, island—and smoother traffic flow.*

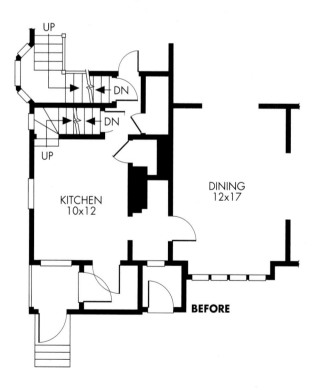

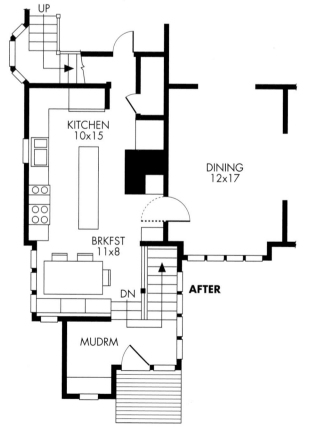

As part of the addition, a cooktop set into a new peninsula allows the cook to face the breakfast room and talk with family or friends.

When the owners added a new kitchen at the rear of the house, they turned former kitchen space into a welcoming hearth-side sitting room.

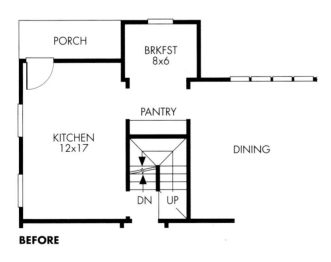

PORCH

BRKFST
8x6

PANTRY

KITCHEN
12x17

DINING

DN   UP

BEFORE

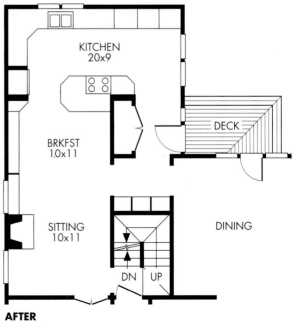

KITCHEN
20x9

DECK

BRKFST
10x11

SITTING
10x11

DINING

DN   UP

AFTER

Make a Wish List

Happily, there's no cost to dreaming on paper. Before calling a builder or an architect, make a wish list of the features you've always wanted, and number them in order of importance. Clip good ideas from magazines and keep them in a folder—they can help you communicate with your builder or architect when the time comes. Then, sketch all the alternative floor plans you can imagine and save your favorites. Here are a few ideas that reflect current remodeling trends:

Kitchens. Opening a kitchen to an adjacent living space is a good place to start, but don't stop there. Create a two-cook kitchen by adding a second sink and separating the cooktop from the oven to make room for two tasks at once. If you plan to add a kitchen or a garage, be sure they are closely linked for easy hauling of groceries.

Great-rooms. If you combine a kitchen and dining area with a comfortable living area focused on a fireplace, you'll be creating a great-room patterned after early American homes. Today's version often features vaulted ceilings.

First-floor master suites. Give your new, main-level master suite privacy and a natural sound barrier by locating it around a corner or down a short hall from main living areas.

▲ The screened back porch added to this Atlanta, Georgia, house offers retreat, refuge, and privacy. New columns provide architectural interest and add to the cordial Southern atmosphere.

Don't Do That

■ Don't build your entry without a closet. Everyone needs a place for coats.

■ Don't always put doors on dining rooms. Carrying food and dishes from your kitchen to the dining room can be easier and safer without them.

■ Don't forget that doors swing. You won't want doors that open into busy hallways, onto glass, or into stairways.

■ Don't put laundry rooms close to public rooms where chugging machines will intrude on conversations with your guests.

■ Don't create awkward traffic patterns. You won't want to force people to walk through a private space, such as a bedroom or home office, to get to a more public space, such as the living room.

▲ Expansive floor-to-ceiling windows draw a fine line between this comfortably furnished porch and a backyard world of blossoms and dogwoods. The handsome floor is made of durable slate.

Surviving the Mess

Before a trio of dormer windows were added, this was an unremarkable ranch house. During the remodeling, a temporary waste chute carried off debris from the roof.

Whether you're tackling the project yourself or bringing in professionals, you'll need a clear plan for handling the mess. If you're hiring a builder, work with him or her to create a detailed cleanup plan. Also, walk contractors through your house to point out what areas must be protected.

Put up dust shields to protect yourself and your furnishings. Saws and sledgehammers will stir up a billowing dust storm that you must contain. To keep your living quarters clean, seal off the project rooms with plastic curtains and duct tape, and remove furniture and electronic equipment from rooms near the project. At the very least, cover furnishings with sheets, plastic wrap, or drop cloths.

Create a trash path. Broken plaster, mounds of insulation, and shards of wood from a single demolished wall can fill an entire room. You'll need to create a wide pathway leading out of the house to the trash bin. Lay down plastic or cardboard to protect interior floors, and put up signs or barriers outside around any prized landscaping. Make sure your trash-removal route steers workers away from living areas.

Plan living arrangements. If possible, move to a motel for a short time, or at least

Consider Kids

Tammy Barnett says the best move she ever made was to leave her husband, Dick. As the couple planned major remodeling of their St. Louis home, they realized they didn't want their two daughters exposed to the mess and danger of an active construction site.

"I took the kids and went to my mother's for more than a month that summer. There was no way I was going to live through that mess with a baby and a toddler," Tammy says.

While they were safely away, Dick coordinated the work of a team of contractors.

"For a couple of weeks, the house looked like a bomb hit it. You can't have a couple of babies in the middle of that mess," Dick says.

He lived in the master bedroom for weeks with a microwave oven, a television, and a VCR.

He says, "I'd work all day at my job and do what I could around here at night. Then, I'd fall in bed late. It was tough, but we all survived the ordeal with the help of Tammy's folks. The results were worth the trauma."

▲ *This living room was expanded with space taken from a former hallway. A wide passageway with a transom window now opens the living area to the dining room. Additional windows invite light to fill this side of the house.*

protect young children from fumes and jagged construction waste by sending them to a relative's house. If you do stay home, consolidate your living quarters so you have a clean, safe area as far away from the mess as possible. Make sure rooms where you live have all the necessary amenities—a phone, a microwave oven, and

bathroom access. You'll need a refrigerator, but instead of lugging your kitchen fridge to the upstairs bedroom, consider renting or purchasing a smaller, portable unit. If water will be shut off for long periods of time, put in an order for bottled water delivery and arrange for showers at the homes of sympathetic friends or relatives.

Working Well with Others

▲ *Good communication is vital to the success of your project. When meeting with your architect or designer, take along your magazine clippings, rough sketches, and product brochures to help express your ideas.*

No matter what the size of your addition, you will undoubtedly be seeking the advice and services of many professionals. You may eventually be talking to bankers, architects, general contractors, members of your city's planning commission, carpenters, plumbers, electricians, interior designers, and others. In order to communicate your ideas effectively, it is helpful to understand how these professionals work, what they charge, and what can be expected of them.

The key co-players will be your architect and general contractor. Or, these services might be combined and offered as a design/build team. Each comes to a job with their own set of professional standards. Here's what you can expect.

Architects

Homeowners often believe that hiring an architect will add unnecessary expense to the project.

However, a good architect who has experience in remodeling projects will often provide creative solutions to difficult problems. The detailed drawings that an architect furnishes will allow the work to proceed smoothly and efficiently—saving money (and heartache) in the process. An architect's standard fee is 10 to 15 percent of a project's budget, but price is usually negotiable. Most architects are willing to act as consultants or to provide partial design solutions; you can customize your relationship with an architect in a number of ways. Some architects offer a two-hour consultation for a few hundred dollars—a small price for high-style dividends.

If your home has any architectural value because of its age or original design, hiring an architect to shape the addition is an especially wise investment. Most architects have a reverence for the past and a good sense of how to make new construction fit in with old. They are also well-versed in current building techniques and the latest building materials.

To find a good architect, get recommendations from friends or check with the American Institute of Architects through local chapters or its headquarters in Washington, D.C. During the initial consultation, look at examples of the architect's work and get a feeling for how they would approach your project.

Design/Builders

Not everyone goes to architectural school to learn design. Design/builders is a relatively new term for general building contractors who both design and build projects. Because these professionals have experience swinging hammers, as well as at the drafting table, their design solutions are often well-integrated with the construction process. The result is a project that is run in a highly efficient manner. Because their design fees are included in their building fees, a design/build team can usually bid a project at a lower price than a separate architect and general contractor.

A design/build team should have a general contractor's license, but may not have a professional designer's accreditation. Their designs must bear the stamp of a structural engineer before work can begin. Ask to see photos of previous projects and for the team to provide references that you can call.

General contractors

When you need someone to run all construction phases of your project, you hire a general contractor. They will oversee the schedule, order all the materials, and provide the subcontractors—carpenters, plumbers, tile setters, etc.—necessary to complete the job. A general contractor with many years of experience in your community is a valuable resource because of his or her familiarity with the work of the area's subcontractors.

The general contractor you hire may swing a hammer, but more likely they will be on the phone making sure that the job progresses smoothly. As with design/builders, you should ask prospective general contractors for bids and a list of references you can call.

▲ *It's the job of the general contractor to schedule subcontractors and arrange for materials to be delivered. If this framing lumber hadn't been at the job site on time, work would have halted.*

Case History

Then there's the story of Nancy and Rod Travers. They decided they could design and build their own addition.

Rod says, "Because Nancy has some interior design training in her background, we thought we were up to the job. Big mistake."

The towering Victorian-era house the couple own needed a modern first floor. Nancy's addition looked great on paper.

But work had only begun when they started discovering miscalculations and wrong measurements. Walls were off-line, floors uneven, and windows slightly out of kilter.

Wisely, the couple sent out a call to professionals to help them out. "You have to admit what you don't know," Nancy says, "particularly with the biggest investment you'll ever make."

Do It Yourself?

Many homeowners enjoy direct involvement with the work process, either doing the labor themselves or acting as their own general contractor and coordinating the work of various subcontractors. This level of involvement can be challenging and highly satisfying. However, it is also demanding and time-consuming. A good knowledge of construction techniques and terminology is required for either type of involvement. Only experienced do-it-yourselfers should consider tackling complex addition projects. If you act as your own general contractor, you will have to make yourself available at regular intervals to answer questions and make decisions.

Acting as general contractor

The idea of acting as a general contractor often appeals to people who are concerned about saving money. They believe that eliminating this position will save funds that will trim the overall budget, or can then be used to upgrade materials or buy furnishings. It's a good theory, and it can work if you have the time and energy to devote to the project. Remember that running a building project is a complex job. You must coordinate work so plumbers, electricians, and others arrive at the moment their skills are needed. Because subcontractors are always juggling several jobs at once, a cancellation because of missed timing may wind up delaying a project for several weeks and costing more money than you planned.

Finding the best subcontractors for your job can be time-consuming. Ask friends and neighbors for recommendations, and if you see (and like) a project that's under construction, stop and ask the homeowner who's doing the work. You'll need bids from two or three companies for each type of assignment, and you'll need to check references. Information from Better Business Bureaus is limited, but it's wise to give them a call, too. The BBB can tell you if any complaints have been filed against a company you may want to hire.

The D-I-Y approach

Few satisfactions match that of working on your own building project with your own hands—and doing it well. You will set your own quality standards, make all decisions, and learn along the way.

As you weigh the option of doing the entire project yourself, honesty is the best policy. Be honest about your knowledge, your skill levels, and your shortcomings. You'll want to create a library of information that relates to your project from books, magazines, and tapes. Take an honest assessment of the time required, and judge accordingly. Even a modest project will probably require several weekends and evenings to complete, along with several unanticipated trips to the hardware store or home supply center.

Your friend—the inspector

Although a visit from a building inspector can cause some moments of anxiety, there is no better ally for the homeowner/general contractor or do-it-yourselfer than the inspector. They will visit the building site as work progresses and poke into every aspect of the job. Their questions are always technical and precise. Your answers must be the same or you can expect a red-tag notice that will shut down the job until corrections are made.

It's important to remember that the building inspector is working in your best interests by helping ensure the safety of you and your family. Often, you can call an inspector to visit your site and check on work in progress, even before a scheduled inspection. Most inspectors appreciate the extra effort you demonstrate toward doing the project correctly and will take the time to advise you about the integrity of your work.

► *Do you have the skill to lay tile, install a whirlpool tub with a motor, mount a faucet, set glass block, build light frames from hardwood, and put down a floor? Then you may be ready for a bathroom do-it-yourself project as complex as the one shown here.*

Build a Team, Then an Addition

As the homeowner, you are the project's leader. You need to develop a clear image of your addition and then transmit that goal to your team of architects, designers, and builders. Everyone on the team must be focused on the same result if the project is to succeed. If you communicate enthusiasm and certainty, the team will feel the same way. This doesn't mean that you have to supply all the ideas. An architect and interior designer may provide many of the concepts that shape your addition. Nor does it mean that everyone will always agree. But differing opinions are often the source of great creativity and imaginative solutions. Ultimately, the decision will be yours.

Assemble your team

Hiring the right workers is a skill. If you personally know contractors or subcontractors with good reputations, then you can proceed with confidence. Otherwise, you'll have to do your homework—seeking recommendations, interviewing prospective builders and tradespeople, and then inspecting their work. The effort you put into this phase of the job should yield a project that proceeds smoothly, and your satisfaction with the results long after the work crew is gone.

Be careful when hiring friends or family, particularly if they are treating your project as a side job. They may come at an attractive price, but it's hard to keep remodeling on a strictly business basis with a brother-in-law or an old buddy. Schedules tend to slide and quality, as well as friendships, can suffer.

Do your bidding

When hiring most contractors, you will ask for bids. Because there are no set fees, you should gather several bids before hiring. In each case, you need to show the plans and explain them in detail. Make sure that all those who are bidding get the same information in the same way.

If a bid seems too high, ask the contractors to explain the rationale for their numbers. It may be that they are including costs that other bidders are trying to hide. For instance, one framing contractor may not include the price of hauling waste from the job while a higher-priced bidder will. In this case, the higher price is more accurate and fair because all expenses are on the table.

Written contracts are needed for each company you hire. Contracts should clearly state who is supplying materials, what those materials are, the date work will be started and completed, how much will be paid, timing of payments, and penalties for missing project deadlines.

Create a schedule

After you have assembled your team, create a master schedule that includes the dates when each category of materials should be on hand and when work will actually begin. If you are acting as your own general contractor, a schedule will help you coordinate critical shipments and avoid delays. If a general contractor is handling the job, be sure to make regular appointments with him or her to handle all decisions you'll need to make to help keep the project on time.

◄ *This home had trend-setting style when it was built in the 1950s, but times had passed it by. Close collaboration with an architect produced this bold entry featuring glass block and large-scale framing.*

▲ *Don't drive down to the home center and expect to find a glass bump-out such as the one used to create this gleaming bath. This addition required planning. It often takes up to 10 weeks to get delivery of a specialty enclosure such as this, so work with your design team to order in a timely manner.*

Building Codes and You

Not all building codes are intended to save lives, but most building regulations are intended to make the house as safe and efficient as possible. Although some regulations are criticized as cumbersome and outdated, or even as impediments to good design, the code system has undoubtedly and dramatically raised the overall quality of the nation's housing.

There is no single code governing the entire nation. Instead, there are several basic building codes for various regions. In addition, states, cities, and counties enact their own codes. Most of the codes apply to new construction, which includes additions or extensive remodeling projects. Although most banks and other lending institutions will not allow a house to be sold if it is in violation of uniform building codes, there is no penalty for living in an older house that has what building inspectors describe as "existing but non-code-conforming" conditions such as old wiring or outdated plumbing.

Building codes evolve as communities experience natural disasters, fires, accidents, environmental difficulties, and failures of the various household systems. For instance, in the wake of killer hurricanes, Florida has been tightening codes governing roofs and siding. Californians are constantly reviewing their earthquake-related codes as their cities are shaken by temblors. And the state of Washington now demands stronger window framing because of repeated damage from high winds and coastal storms. All of these code changes affect both new-home construction and the building of additions.

Construction rules are also shaped by new building technologies and products entering the market. This happened in the late 1980s as direct-vent gas fireplaces became popular. Some regions resisted these burners because their chimney systems are made with insulated pipes small enough to fit inside a wall. Some building codes specifically banned these devices until the safety of this technology could be proven to skeptical fire officials.

Environmental concerns are having a significant impact on codes, too. Revamped rules dictate the amount of water your new toilet can consume with each flush, designate the efficiency level of your new gas furnace, control the type of paint you can use on your walls, and govern a host of other aspects when remodeling.

Codes also continue their traditional role of defining how a structure will be built—from the depth of foundation footings to the distance between wall studs to the amount of flashing needed along roof valleys to keep water out. In each of these instances, building codes serve the homeowner well. As building inspectors arrive at your home to make certain each regulation is met, they assure the owners that work is proceeding properly and that you will be snug and warm for many winters to come.

▲ *When built, the home's back wall ran right behind the sink, and there was no breakfast room beyond. There is still a terrific view of the outdoors from the sink, but there's also additional living space.*

▲ *Thanks to picture-perfect windows and double skylights, this Portland, Oregon, breakfast room addition captures all of the light anyone could want. The 10×12-foot room was built off the end of the kitchen. Building codes governed such issues as how windows were framed and the size of the ceiling beam.*

Start with the Structure

Every part of your home needs a thorough inspection before you begin serious planning for an addition. Inspections begin at the foundation and include the structural components as well as the major systems—electrical, plumbing, and heating and cooling. An inspection will help determine if any part of your house needs upgrading to accommodate the addition. For example, an expanded kitchen might require new electrical circuits to handle additional lights and appliances. You also might find out if it's time to replace corroded plumbing or add more insulation to the existing portion of your home. With an inspection, you'll be able to make an accurate accounting of the total financial impact of your remodeling project.

Consider hiring a pro. Unless you have adequate experience and knowledge, it's best to pay a home inspection service. Inspection requires agility and a broad knowledge of building techniques and equipment. Proceed by yourself only if you have adequate experience and knowledge. Look for inspection services in the local telephone book. Expect to pay about $200–$300 for an inspection of an average-size suburban home.

Following are some of the items that need to be evaluated during an inspection.

Roof. Are angles, edges, and valleys tight and straight, or do they sag? Are shingles or other roofing materials in good condition?

Siding. Look for evidence of water or insect invasion under the siding.

Foundation. Look closely around both the exterior and interior foundation for cracks, loose material, or signs of water damage. Also check for signs that the house is settling unevenly.

Chimney. Check for any sign of loose bricks and put a level on the chimney to see if the structure remains straight. Inside, be sure that the fireplace draws well. For safety's sake, check to see if it needs to be swept.

Gutters. Be sure gutters are free of holes and that they are not sagging. Do downspouts carry water well away from your home's foundation?

Windows and doors. Do they open and close easily and smoothly? Is the paint in good shape? Are there any old, single-pane windows that should be replaced with energy-saving glass?

Floors. Are your floors level and free of major squeaks? Are the subfloor and its supporting joists in solid shape? Also check that the flooring material itself is in good condition.

Kitchen. Inspect the area beneath kitchen cabinets to make sure water hasn't invaded. Locate plumbing pipes and vents and see if they fit into your new kitchen arrangement. Plumbing wall changes can become expensive. If you are keeping some cabinets, check to be sure that drawer fronts are securely affixed and that doors hang squarely.

Bathroom. Plumbing should be in working order. Check for water damage around fixtures.

Interior rooms. Walk through other rooms to make certain everything is level and straight.

Tools to Use

Load up your tool belt if you're going to inspect the house yourself. Here are some of the tools and safety gear you'll need:

■ A level at least 36 inches long to help you check floors and counters.

■ A metal pry bar for lifting siding (also for pulling away cobwebs).

■ A tape measure at least 25 feet long.

■ A framing square so you can make sure walls and floors are properly aligned. This tool looks like two metal yardsticks welded together at a 90-degree angle.

■ A ladder so you can reach the roof.

■ Heavy clothes, gloves, and safety goggles for your protection.

■ A good respirator with filters to protect you against inhaling any hazardous particles in basements and attics.

▲ *This living room was a confining little box before it was opened up with a cathedral ceiling and a wall of windows. Opening this space to the adjacent dining area makes it seem even bigger.*

Home Work

Over, under, sideways, down. Those are just a few of the positions you'll be in if you decide to do a general home inspection yourself instead of hiring a professional.

You will be crawling under the house, scaling its walls, poking through the attic, and climbing on the roof. Be certain that you are wearing appropriate clothes, including gloves and safety goggles. Keep a respirator close because you may need it when you descend into the bowels of your house. Guard yourself against breathing in old paint dust, asbestos fibers, and other toxics.

The length of your checklist will be determined by the kind of addition you are tackling. Focus your inspection efforts on the areas of your present structure that will be affected. Our checklist (*opposite*) covers most of the items you may need to inspect and correct before remodeling gets under way.

Begin the inspection by noting the measurements of the house and the types of materials used. Along the way, note such items as window sizes, dimension of framing materials, type of roofing, and makeup of the siding.

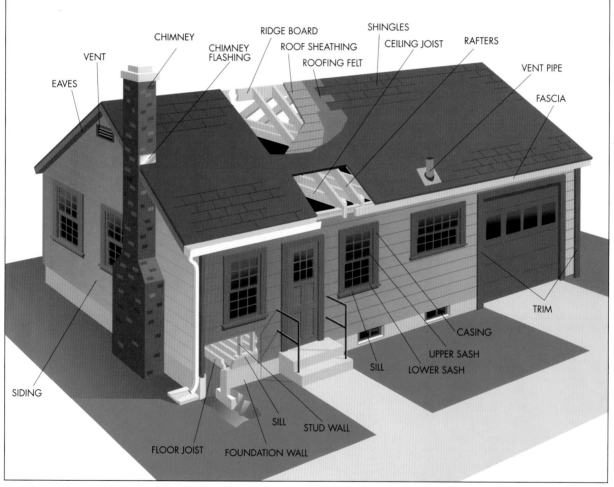

▲ *Fluency in the language of house construction is necessary if you are handling most aspects of the project yourself. If you talk to subcontractors about "rafters" when you mean "joists," you are turning your remodeling on its head. This diagram illustrates some basic home-building jargon. It's worthwhile to familiarize yourself with these common terms so that you can communicate well with your project team.*

Inspection Checklist

	Good	Unacceptable

Foundation/Basement Condition
- Water damage ....
- Insect/termites ....
- Settling/crumbling ....
- Rotting ....
- Cracks ....
- Siding ....
- Discoloring.........................
- Deterioration/damage ....

Roof Condition
- Flashing ....
- Gutters...............................
- Vents ....

Chimney Condition
- Masonry ....
- Liner and cap ....

Attic Condition
- Water damage ....
- Rafters ....
- Insulation ....

Windows Condition
- Frame ....
- Glass ....

Doors Condition
- Frame ....
- Threshold.............................

Trim Condition
- Deterioration/damage ....

Plumbing Condition
- Sagging, leaking, patched pipes......................
- Water pressure ....
- Drains adequately ....
- Fixtures ....

Electrical Condition
- Wiring ....
- Fuse box.............................
- Outlets ....

Heating/Cooling Condition
- Odors or fumes ....
- Sealed and insulated ducts ......
- Odd noises ....

Interior Rooms Condition
- Water damage ....
- Signs of fire ....
- Bulging or bowed walls ....
- Level, firm floors ....
- Fixtures ....

Exploring Solutions

In the pages ahead we'll look at many different ways to add on and how each kind of addition offers creative solutions for your home and family.

Some add on. Others add up. A few even add under. Whatever approach homeowners take when building additions, the one thing they all have in common is a desire to expand the living space of a house.

There are modest additions, such as bump-outs, that add only a few square feet but can dramatically transform a room with light and livability. Other additions can be quite large—wings, second stories, or towers that create space for several bedrooms, new great-rooms that are truly great, or elaborate complexes designed for a variety of uses.

As you consider the possibilities, keep an eye out for relatively simple and cost-effective solutions. An attic dormer, for example, may be all you need to create that peaceful home office you've always envisioned.

➤ *To blend this dining room addition into the existing architecture, the owners of this Iowa home copied a fan pattern seen above the original windows on the front of the house.*

➤ *Dark rooms are a problem with many older homes. Here, a bright dining room addition gives the whole house a sunny lift—and a panoramic view.*

Dormers and Bay Windows

Small additions are a good way to revitalize parts of your home without breaking your budget or creating a major inconvenience for you or your family. But even a modest project can dramatically open up cramped floor space, bring in the view, and admit a welcome wash of light.

Creating dormers is a relatively low-cost way to add livability to any upper-level room that's pinched by low ceilings, short on natural light, or in need of ventilation. Dormers are often used to add space to attic areas with pitched roofs.

For your dormer to be a success, you'll probably need an architect or skilled designer to blend the new structure with the old, particularly if

➤ *An upper-story room can come to life with dormer windows that let in light and air and create more headroom.*

▲ *The addition of light was a primary goal of this remodeling. Dormers helped let sunshine into the upper story; a bump-out gathers light at the entry level.*

DESIGN DETAIL

Architects say that windows are the eyes of the house. By adding a dormer, you've raised those eyes rather dramatically. So make sure you have an illustration drawn that shows how your home's new exterior will look. Renderings used to be done by architects and artists. Now there are computer programs that create future facades in a flash.

Use the addition of a dormer or dormers as an excuse to reinvigorate, remodel, and repaint. Seize the moment to refresh your entire house.

▲ *A prefabricated bay window unit allows the corner of this kitchen to come alive with plants and flowers. The additional light and bigger view expands the feeling of space in this room, too.*

the addition will be on the front of the house. Dormers are usually built on the site with windows, roofing, and siding selected to match your home's existing materials.

Bay windows are other small-addition favorites usually used to give kitchens, dining rooms, or eating areas an extra measure of style and natural light. Because a bay window is usually three-sided, it provides a wide sill that is an excel-

lent place for light-loving plants to thrive. In living rooms, bays can also be used to make room for window seats, which are regaining popularity as today's hectic pace sends us scurrying for solitude and relaxation.

Although bays can be built from three or more individual windows, manufacturers now make one-piece models that are easier to install than those completely built on site.

Bump-Outs

For some, a jetted spa tub is the image of true luxury. Others want a special place to watch the sun come up while they enjoy a light breakfast. Still others want to entertain, but their dining room seems too tight. Bump-outs may be the answer in each situation.

Bump-outs are relatively small additions that can have big impact on how a room functions and feels. They expand a room by moving walls out only a few feet. Although the exterior of the house will change, the smallest bump-outs can

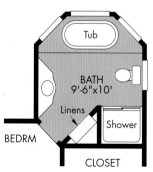

▲ *A four-foot bump-out put this whirlpool tub at center stage and transformed a modest little bath into a wonderful suite. The three-sided addition allows for a sweeping view of nearby hills.*

usually be built without major (and costly) changes to the foundation or roof.

Begin planning by preparing a floor-plan diagram of the entire room and the proposed bump-out. How does the bump-out you envision fit into the room's layout? Will it accommodate any furnishings you plan to place in it? Will the bump-out interfere with any passageways? Will the new space feel balanced? If you plan well, your bump-out will not only fit your space, but it also will dramatically improve it visually.

Next, make a close inspection of the area where the bump-out will be attached. Pay close attention to the roof and area where any foundation footings will be placed in the ground. Save money by tucking the roof of the bump-out under the eaves of the existing roof. If you have to tie a new roof section into the existing one, expect more cost and complexity. Sometimes an entire roof must be replaced because the new section makes the older part look dated.

Because you will ripping an opening into an existing wall to make way for the bump-out, you need to determine what's inside the wall cavity before swinging a sledge into it. Will remodeling disturb electric wires or plumbing lines? Make plans to reroute those services, if necessary. Also, you or your builder should consult a structural engineer about the need for any new supporting beams that may be required to keep the walls and ceiling firmly in place. This is no time to play amateur engineer; hire a pro to tell you if the load-bearing walls need any extra support to keep the roof from caving in.

As new walls go up, they will have to be sided in a way that enhances the exterior siding already on the house. But this doesn't mean the addition has to exactly match walls around it. Instead, many new rooms make their mark by playing off other elements of the existing structure. For instance, a clapboard-sided addition can perk up a brick structure if the millwork mimics other wood trim already attached to the house. Likewise, a brick addition can give a wood-sided house some flair. (To see a mix of exterior materials in action, see the home on pages 76 and 77.)

Regardless of the exterior materials, keep comfort and energy in mind as you build. Fill walls with generous amounts of insulation. If yours is an especially small bump-out with no foundation—one bolted to the house with joist hangers—be sure to insulate the floor as well.

Consider how the new structure's appearance impacts your exterior, too. Windows can be too big and they can be the wrong style (double-hung instead of casements, for instance). New installations should match existing windows.

Finally, examine the interior finishes you have now and consider the bump-out's impact. For instance, if your house has older lath-and-plaster walls, a contemporary drywall treatment on the bump-out may not look right. Matching the floor presents similar issues. If yours is a small bumped-out bay, consider adding a window seat to conceal the junction of new and old floors.

DESIGN DETAIL

If you are thinking of creating a bump-out, consider these design opportunities:

■ If it's a dining room bump-out, a low buffet could be used to draw attention toward a spectacular view.

■ Give a master bedroom a sitting spot and a fresh focal point by adding a windowed, bumped-out bay.

■ Family room bump-outs often become the focal point of the room. Fill them with a direct-vent gas fireplace or a grand new entertainment center. In the later case, putting up new walls allows you to install sophisticated new wiring required for advanced electronics.

■ Entry bump-outs can be a wonderful addition to snow-country houses. They increase space for your cold-weather gear and can be tied into your home's heating-duct system.

■ In a bath, set the windows high enough so you can stand in the tub looking out—but the view of those looking toward the house from outside is blocked. Or, gain privacy by adding half-panels of sheers or shutters.

Whole Room Additions

When there's no room in your home anymore, the best remedy may be to add a room—a bedroom suite, a home office, or a family room. This is an excellent opportunity to change the character of your home and how you live, so expect to spend weeks or even months of preparing for a successful room project.

Get design help. Because a room addition is a complex undertaking, it's a good idea to consult an architect or other qualified design professional. Architects and their design counterparts have the skills to shape the new room so it flows easily into the existing mix of rooms. The challenge may be one of simply blending the new room into the rest of the house

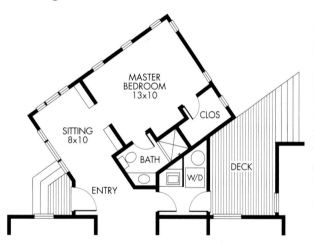

▲ *By angling this room addition away from the house slightly, its impact on the existing home's foundation, roof, and exterior walls was minimized.*

or of using the addition and a few other modifications to give your home a fresh look. During discussions with your architect or designer, look for ways to add interesting interior architecture that will give the room a distinct personality. The project is an opportunity to add drama—to create an expansive window wall, add skylights, or alter the ceiling height.

Although most room additions are designed to suit a particular home, many contracting companies offer package deals, which include the design, materials, and labor for the job. Buying

such an "off-the-shelf" addition can be a good move if your concern is focused more on your budget than your architecture. But beware of packages that offer no more style than a shoebox. Also, look out for packages that keep costs in check by selling you poor windows, hollow doors, and minimal insulation.

Build your team. Adding a new room will involve major construction, so be prepared to put a whole team together for the project (see pages 22–23). A room addition will require you to create a huge hole through an existing wall to link the new and old rooms, and shoring up that area may require the calculations of an engineer. Be sure to talk with your contractor about keeping that area of your home secure. Most builders will seal the hole with a temporary covering of plywood that is removed each work morning.

An additional room will also require new foundation footings, electrical service, or plumbing. It is also usually impossible to avoid disturbing the existing roof, part of which may need to be replaced in the process. A skilled roofing contractor will ensure a tight seal where the new roof connects to the existing one. You or your contractor should ask all bidders for a detailed description of their approach to this part of the job.

DESIGN DETAIL

Add another professional to your project team: a lighting designer whose skills can shed light on good design to make rooms function better and more efficiently.

Only lighting-industry insiders can keep up with advancing technology. But you don't have to understand cool lighting vs. warm lighting, halogen vs. fluorescent, or the advantages of low-voltage lighting. A knowledgeable designer can inform you.

Check with lighting specialty stores for pros who can design lighting schemes—not just sell you fixtures and bulbs.

▲ *A selection of warm-toned wood and a matching fir beam stretched over a passageway add architectural interest to these rooms in Seattle. Overhead, a large skylight informs the entryway with a wash of welcoming natural light.*

➤ *It might have been easier to install a single large window for this sitting area. But this fanciful window arrangement is far more appealing and fun.*

Front-Yard Additions

Although it's more common to look to the side or rear of the house when adding on, don't overlook the possibilities that the front of your house may offer. Done right, such a project will not only add space but curb appeal, too.

Adding a room at the front can transform the entire house, as demonstrated by the double-gable living room project on these pages. In this case, the addition was prompted by a growing Chicago-area family's desire to continue living in a shady, stable neighborhood, despite their home's small size. Fortunately, theirs was one of the most modestly sized homes in the area, so

▲ *Building codes governing the building of stairwells are quite strict and specific. Make sure you understand the rules, as these homeowners did.*

◀ *From the outside, the round window appears to be a vintage design element. But inside— surrounded by contemporary decorating details—it makes the living room seem more stylish than ever.*

▲ *If there are mature trees such as these on your lot, they should be protected. Holding this addition back a few feet helped preserve healthy trees as an investment in the environment and the value of the property.*

DESIGN DETAIL

When you add a signature element, such as the round window seen in the photograph (*left*), it should also be a neat design fit. Such elements should never:

■ Draw undue attention to themselves. The round window here isn't so large it overwhelms the surrounding design.

■ Be positioned so they intrude. Although this window floats high in the gable, more than half of the circle is below the upper piece of white trim. As a result, the gable still stands out on its own.

■ Violate the vintage feel of a home. The round window blends with the architecture.

expanding the structure did not threaten to increase the house's value beyond what would be reasonable for the neighborhood.

With an architect's help, the couple created a design that added a great deal of personal style and much-needed living space to their older home. Now, a spacious entry allows a gentle transition from the outside to the inside, replacing an entry that originally led guests directly from the front steps into the living room. The house was extended into the front yard, but the project still met local set-back requirements.

This addition beautifully illustrates how an addition can fit the exterior of an older home while updating the flow of space inside. Viewing the house from the street, it would be difficult to guess that the front section is an addition; the siding, windows, front door, trim, and even the roof pitches all seem to flow seamlessly from another time period. Similarly, inside the home, the blocky style of the staircase, wood floors, and the paneled closet door point to an older age. But the open floor plan—and even the vaulted ceiling—met the homeowners' decidedly modern-day needs and aesthetics.

Of course, a front addition doesn't necessarily have to be a living room. It could be a hobby or craft room, a larger dining room, or a home office. In fact, the front of the house is an excellent place for an office addition, especially if you plan to hold business meetings there.

To gain ideas and inspiration for your front-of-house addition, take walking tours of your neighborhood and other areas that were built about the same time. Look for houses that are similar to yours and study how they dealt with rooflines, window choices, entrance schemes, and even landscaping. Consider hiring an architect to help you blend your addition into your existing facade and floor plan.

Second-Story Additions

▲ *This dramatic, steeply pitched ceiling is a tribute to the skills and imaginations of the homeowners, the architect, and the drywall installers. Remember that building codes govern such things as the height of walls, so unusually low side walls such as these may require special permission from building inspectors.*

Second-floor additions can yield exciting results, both inside and out, but they also are the most challenging of construction projects. In fact, building a new house is usually an easier assignment than capping a one-story structure with another story. So, why consider it? You may have no other choice if your lot is so small that a ground-floor addition would push walls too close to property lines. Also, creating a second story has certain cost advantages—if your foundation footings are large enough to handle the load, you will not have to alter or add on to your existing foundation. In the example shown above, a Colorado family capped a ho-hum garage with a stunning second-story guest room, complete with a dramatic window wall.

Before proceeding with a second-story addition, a structural engineer must make certain that the existing walls and foundation can support the weight of the addition. This specialist's advice will be vital as you estimate costs, because shoring up weak walls can be costly.

◄ *On this new second story, a pair of eyebrow dormers repeats the angle of the home's original gable. New porch details pull the facade together.*

Photographer, Caroline B. Bergs

▼ *Before the addition went up, the central section seemed tacked on to the two-story part of the house.*

If you decide to go ahead with your plans, you also will need to consult an architect or other qualified design professional. All construction is scrutinized when you are seeking building permits. But you can expect an even more detailed examination for this kind of project. Government agencies will ask for detailed blueprints, as well as documentation from the structural engineer.

Also, you'll want to consult with a heating and cooling contractor. Heating this type of addition is often manageable because warm air will rise to the second floor without a great deal of help, assuming that your furnace can handle the new load. But cooling is another matter. You'll want expert help with decisions about heating-and-cooling equipment and ducting. In some cases it's best, both in terms of installation and monthly utility costs, to give a new, second-floor space its own heating and cooling system. Also, contact local utility companies. Some offer low-interest financing of the latest high-efficiency equipment, and payments for the equipment may become part of the monthly bill.

Don't forget to seek the advice of a plumber. You'll save money if you can stack a new second-story bathroom above existing plumbing lines and drains. In the second-floor addition shown above, a new bathroom was positioned directly on top of the one on the first floor.

DESIGN DETAIL

A second-story addition will usually require a staircase. In times past, that meant hiring a carpenter to build it at the site.

But you can purchase stairs today from manufacturers who build one thing: stairs. Factory-built stairs will generally offer more years of trouble-free service because they are built in a controlled environment by people with plenty of staircase experience. They know how to banish squeaks.

Specialty manufacturers are also the place to go for spiral staircases made from wood or metal.

Two-Story Additions

If the time has come for your house to expand to meet the needs of your growing family, a two-story addition may be an ideal solution. Two-story additions permit you to reconfigure both levels of your two-story house at the same time. One advantage to this type of addition is that there is a certain conservation of materials and labor involved. That is, because you are building up and not just out, the size of your new foundation and the square footage of your new roof will be relatively modest. Two-story additions are ideal if:

■ Property line set-backs will not allow your house to sprawl.

■ The size of the house when it is completed will still be appropriate when compared to other houses in the neighborhood.

■ Moving is out of the question.

The family whose house is shown on these pages faced just such a situation when a grandmother with Alzheimer's disease was going to move in with them. After weighing all the options, they decided to build a two-story addition at the rear of their home to make an apartment for their mother. Their new space has a bedroom with a small built-in kitchen and a sunny sitting room. The reconfiguration also added space to other rooms and resulted in major changes to the overall floor plan of the house—a bonus for everyone as the house became bigger and more relaxed.

In this case, the back wall of the home came off to make way for the addition. But this isn't always necessary. Towers are sometimes built near the main house and linked to it by a short ground-level passageway or bridge. With this approach, demolition work and the disruption it causes are limited. Costs can also be lower because there's no need to tear into containing electric lines, plumbing pipes, venting stacks, and chimneys. Moving any of these services will probably become expensive.

In cases where a two-story addition will stand somewhat separate from the existing home, erecting the addition will differ only marginally from building a new home. There may not be as many rooms as in a new house—you may not be putting in a kitchen, for instance—but the addition will have a separate foundation and its own electrical, plumbing, and heating and air-conditioning (HVAC) systems.

Designing an addition this large will probably require the services of an architect. A skilled architect will be able to match the architectural style of your addition with your existing structure, mimicking siding, window styles, and roof lines. Often, an addition of this type can actually improve the lines of a house.

Because these additions can be quite tall, you may have views you've never really seen from your present house. During planning, find out what vistas you have the opportunity to gain by climbing up a large ladder on the spot where the addition will stand so you can survey the view. Don't be surprised if you climb back down with a desire to increase window sizes.

DESIGN DETAIL

If you plan on installing wood floors, consider putting down planks made from unusual species of antique, salvaged wood rather than new wood. There are many smaller, reputable companies who scout out sources for old wood and then mill their finds into fine flooring. They recycle pecan from old factory floors, rock maple from bowling alleys, and heart pine from logs found on lake and river bottoms. Many of the species they offer are no longer commercially logged.

Lumberyards and larger home centers can usually obtain this wonderful wood.

▲ Heeding the traditional look of vintage solariums and sleeping porches—and clad to match the rest of the house—this new two-story addition looks as if it's always been there.

◄ With its vintage-style windows and nostalgic wicker, the second-floor sunroom fits beautifully into the original house and gives its owners a fresh peek into the treetops.

Wing Additions

▲ *Skillful blending of architectural styles keeps this wing in tune with the original. The gable-end structure with the chimney is the existing cottage. The section of the house to the right is the wing addition.*

Today's trends find that wing additions often include kitchens that open onto great-rooms. By including these rooms in their addition, homeowners can shape them the way they want to. They can push up the ceilings, lasso light with windows and skylights, and finally have enough room for the big dinner parties they have always wanted. Imaginations aren't limited by the shape of the original portion of the home. Wings are also often used to create new master suites, a reconfiguration of space that frees up the former master bedroom for a variety of uses.

The first challenge of building a wing is to make sure your plans meet local set-back requirements. These laws often affect the shape and design of wing additions. You'll also want to know what additional requirements your wing will make on electrical, plumbing, and heating and air conditioning systems. If the new wing is extensive, you may want to install a separate HVAC system to handle the load. Your architect, general contractor, or design/build team should be able to provide you with the

◀ *This wing addition doubled the size of the house—from 1,400 square feet to 2,800 square feet—at a cost of about $80 per square foot. The homeowners gained a combined living and dining space, with a master suite above.*

MASTER BEDRM 17x12

BATH

OPEN

DN

BEDRM 13x10

HALL

DN

BATH

BEDRM 13x10

HOT TUB

STOR

CARPORT

COURTYARD

LIVING/DINING 27x17

DN

LIBRARY/STUDY 22x6

UP

W/D

LAUN

BATH

MECH

CLOS

ENTRY

KIT/BRKFST 13x21

UP

HALL

GUEST/ STUDY 10x10

MEDIA RM 12x13

answers to all your questions about extending systems and their costs. If you are acting as your own general contractor, you'll want to make careful inquiries about these changes with your subcontractors as you are discussing bids.

Wings also offer the opportunity to restyle your landscaping. If the addition is attached to the rear of the home, you may have a natural courtyard in the crook between the old and new. This can be an ideal place for a covered porch or sunroom. Those who entertain frequently can extend their parties into this space so the entire home seems even larger and more relaxed.

▲ *Deep recesses for the hearth and the windows give the impression that the house was built with thick masonry walls. But it was conventionally framed and finished.*

◄ *The new wing is connected to the kitchen with a wide hallway. In the old and new spaces, there is room to entertain 60 guests.*

DESIGN DETAIL

The area where your wing addition will be connected to your existing house offers many creative possibilities. Some ideas to consider:

■ It could become the home's main entry, if placed at the front of the house. Develop this into a friendly way-station for those coming in or going out. It can replace an entry that is cramped and unflattering.

■ Some passages become display areas. This is a good place to show off family mementos, trophies, or interesting collectibles.

■ Gardeners may discover this to be a great location for a planting counter, particularly if the passage has immediate access to outside. Put large windows in the wall here where you can hang a flower box and lay down a floor of flagstone or slate for a natural feel that cleans up easily and is resistant to water spills.

■ A laundry could find a home here, if the passage is wide enough. Nestled between the main house and the wing, this location could help cut out excessive wash-day travel.

Unusual Additions

The preceding pages touched on most common approaches to constructing additions, but there are still more alternatives. If you have a sloping lot and do not have a full basement, you might build underneath your house and create a walk-out addition. If you own a piece of property with an older, unused structure such as a barn or shed, you may be able to recondition that structure and use it to form the basis of a one-of-a-kind house that is full of personality and character.

Here is a closer look at each of these other types of additions that might fit your situation:

Below grade. What separates a below-grade addition from a regular basement? Light. These types of additions are also called walk-out or daylight basements because they are added beneath homes built on sloping lots. The addition tucks under the existing house and is open to the outside by an abundance of glass; thus, sliding glass doors are a favorite here. The quality of light and the access to the outside opens a world of possibilities for creating an extra bedroom, a home office, or even a teen or mother-in-law apartment with its own private entrance.

Creating a walkout involves removing the soil beside the foundation on the side of the house that has the lower grade, usually at the back of the house. Heavy equipment, such as a backhoe and possibly a dump truck, will be needed for the job, so providing access to your property and protecting your lot and landscaping should be a primary concern. Also, an engineer and surveyor will be an important part of your construction team.

Two important issues accompany building this kind of addition: the need for a ceiling surface and cutting in stairs to the first floor of the existing house. An 8-foot ceiling is needed for comfort in the lower room, but 9 feet is even better. As for the stairs, keep in mind the space you will lose when you build the upstairs stairwell entry and landing. Draw out the plan precisely to make certain the sacrifice is worth it.

Pieced together. It's hard to believe that the top half of the pleasant home shown *opposite* was once a one-vehicle garage housing a yellow school bus. The wooden bus barn was built in the 1930s but had been abandoned for years.

The possibility of putting up a house on this desirable site along a stream motivated the builder to piece together this unusual house. By including the site's original structure within the new design plans, construction was allowed on a piece of property where it would have otherwise been forbidden.

The project began with the pouring of a new foundation designed to perfectly match the footprint of the barn, but about 10 feet to the side of it. Then, the owner erected new 8-foot walls open to the sky on that foundation. Finally, he unbolted the barn from its moorings, lifted the structure with a crane, and set it atop the open wall system of the new house. By wrapping both new and old construction with the same aluminum siding, the house now appears to be one unit built at one time.

Don't Do That

When building an addition, watch out for these common mistakes:

■ Don't build with "green" lumber, just because it was inexpensive to buy. This kind of lumber has not been thoroughly dried and may bow or warp as it dries within your walls. Use only kiln-dried framing lumber.

■ Don't piece together a project with second-hand plywood. Sheets usually come with a grading stamp that guarantees integrity when used correctly. Make sure you have the right plywood for the job (see the Appendix on page 110).

■ Don't let mistakes go as "close enough." A subfloor that's uneven can result in a ridge that tiles can break on; a slightly curved wall will be revealed as unsightly gaps when cabinets are installed, and outlets mounted too low may awkwardly overlap floor molding.

▲ *Unless they watched this house being built, no one can tell that part of this home was once an aging bus barn. The older structure was placed atop a new first level to create this delightful cottage.*

Creating a Floor Plan

Time to get out your pencils and start putting your new addition down on paper. But first you need to diagram the dimensions and floor plan of your house as it presently stands.

In the box provided here—or on separate graph paper or a computer—create an illustration of your present floor plan. It's important to keep your drawing in scale, so carefully measure all rooms and hallways before you begin. Also note the location of any fixture that might be affected by the construction of your addition, such as windows, toilets, tubs, and cabinets.

After you've put your present floor plan on paper, draw it as you hope it will look once the addition is built. Keep in mind the relationships of various rooms, placement of fixtures, and paths of hallways. Don't forget to sketch in the placement of your furniture. Does everything work?

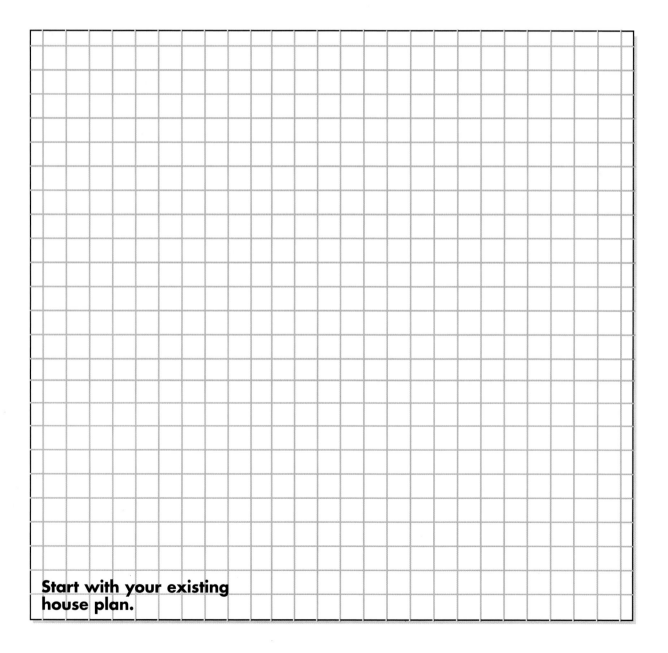

Start with your existing house plan.

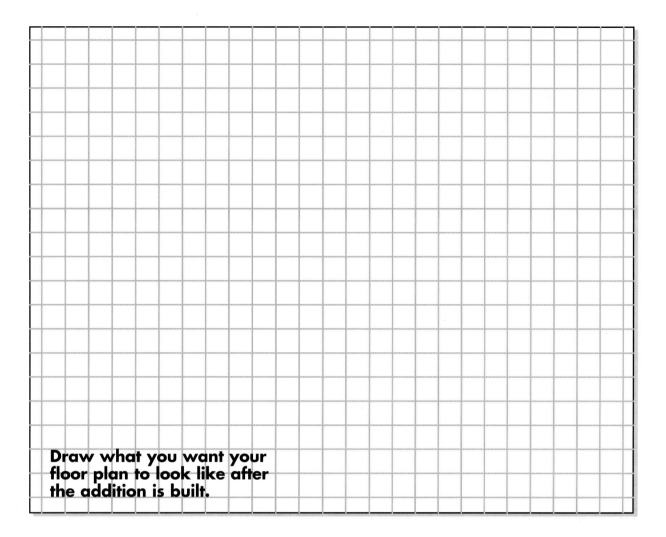

Draw what you want your floor plan to look like after the addition is built.

CREATING A WISH LIST

To get everything you want out of your addition, make up a wish list to guide your design efforts. These questions will help you shape your vision:

■ What do you like best about the present arrangement of the floor plan?

■ What do you like least about it?

■ Which rooms, if any, are too small?

■ Which rooms, if any, are too dark?

■ If money were not an issue, would your kitchen be in the same location? Does its present layout isolate the cook?

■ Does the layout of your home allow you to entertain as comfortably as you would like?

■ Should your living room be a place for daily family activities or a retreat for adult conversation and entertaining?

■ Is the master bedroom arranged to meet your needs, with large closets and enough space in the bathroom?

■ Is there a dining room and is it adequate?

■ When the weather is nice, do you find yourself dreaming about a sunroom or large covered porch?

■ What changes would your house need to make it comfortable and stylish for the next 20 years?

A Closer Look

You've established a general plan for the addition, but there are still details of style and substance to work through.

Creating an addition is an excellent opportunity to enhance the style, comfort, and practicality of your home. You should take the time to carefully plan the details of your new space so that the results will be as satisfying as possible.

In the pages ahead, we'll more closely examine ways in which your design can achieve all these goals, and we'll answer some common questions of style—How important is the architectural style of a home? Why does one house have style and another doesn't seem to have a clue? Is good design only for the rich?

There are also practical matters to consider, such as the best ways to efficiently organize your project, and how to handle elements such as windows and plumbing while maintaining your home's style.

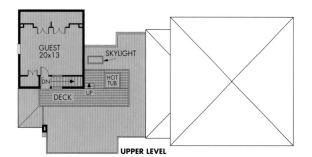

The darker shaded areas of the floor plan (left) reveal that this home doubled in size with a two-story addition. By using the same color brick and continuing the home's strong horizontal lines (right), the addition is a natural fit.

Elements of Good Design

There's a quiet residential street near the ocean in San Juan Capistrano, California, that is lined with the kind of vaguely Spanish-style homes you'd expect to see in this region. Facades have been finished to mimic adobe, and most are capped with red tile roofs. It all seems pleasantly, if somewhat predictably, fitting.

Then—smack in the middle of this Mediterranean milieu—stands a big red saltbox. What is this bit of New England doing here?

The owner explains that she has always loved this style of house, so when her family attained the financial capability to build it, they did. The fact that it is completely out of sync with the neighborhood doesn't bother her at all. Her West Coast home is an almost flawlessly updated version of historic homes seen throughout the East Coast and it is exactly how she envisioned it.

There are lessons here for those who are putting additions on their homes. It raises questions about the appropriateness of a markedly different style plunked down within a monotone neighborhood. It's a question that will gain importance when the eccentric house is sold someday. Certainly, there are buyers who will eagerly request to take tours of such a house. But will they be willing to sign on the dotted line and hand over a check?

As you add on, keep such questions in mind. Your home was built with a particular style—be it a fine Georgian mansion or a simple 1960s ranch. Each of these styles has its own architectural signatures and elements. When it comes to creating an appropriate design for your addition, your existing architecture should offer strong clues about how to proceed.

Today, people are more sophisticated and educated about architecture styles than ever before, thanks to detailed information that appears in magazines, books, newspapers, and even movies. These resources can help you identify architectural styles and the kinds of doors, windows, roofs, and other elements of design that will help your addition blend readily with your existing home. Before beginning your addition, you may want to explore these types of references so that you can make informed decisions about style and design. Making the right design choices will also help protect your investment by keeping your addition in tune with the style of the surrounding neighborhood.

Other elements of good design include:
- The right materials. Any home should be a graceful blend of materials, and the ones you select for the exterior of your home don't necessarily have to match. A variety of materials, such as wood, brick, and stone, will work well together if they complement your home's architecture and if carefully selected for texture and color.
- An elegant proportion. A successful addition will have roof lines and architectural details similar to the original portion of the house. If you are working with an architect, be sure to voice your objections to any design elements that seem inappropriate or awkward. Most architects enjoy working with clients who take an active interest in getting the right results.

Don't Do That

Here are design decisions to avoid:
- Deciding that your staid Greek Revival or other classical design needs to get hip with a contemporary addition. If you want contemporary style, consider a move to a house of more modern design.
- Letting a sale or auction dictate the color of your house. You may get a great price on paint, but if the color is grape purple or sunflower yellow, you may get incredibly strong reactions from friends and neighbors.
- Refusing to invest a few dollars in mullions for replacement windows. If existing windows have true divided lights, any additional windows should imitate their pattern.
- Replacing a fine slate roof with asphalt shingles. If cost is a problem, investigate replacement materials made of cast concrete.

▲ When this Tudor cottage was given a new side porch, the pitch of the porch roof followed that of the existing roof. The result is a look with more balance and appeal than the original design.

➤ Before the porch addition and other remodeling changes were made, this cottage looked much as it did when it was built in the 1920s. Deep overhangs gave the entry a dark appearance.

A Few Rules of Good Taste

▲ *This Connecticut farmhouse reaches out to visitors like a warm embrace. The diagram (right) shows where a sweeping new porch addition was built.*

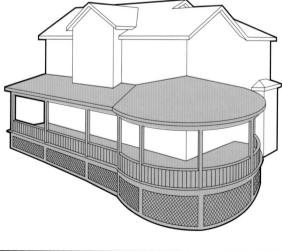

Good taste in home design is usually a balance of ideas—the right color, some pleasing lines, interesting patterns and texture, a sensible fit, and emotional appeal. Your project will be as successful as the one shown on these pages if it incorporates as many of these elements as possible.

Color. Painting the porch white might seem like an obvious choice, but selecting a dark forest green for the lattice screen around the base helps give emphasis to the structure above. The house has a stately simplicity; columns and rails reflect the same qualities.

Lines. Strong horizontal lines run along the face of the porch at floor and ceiling. Notice, too, how the columns seem to be extended all the way to the ground by white trim boards. These lines are tasteful because they lend clarity and certainty to the overall design. But the world isn't only straight lines, so the porch was softened with the gazebo-like section bumped out at one end.

Pattern. The inclusion of the lattice was an inexpensive way to put some pattern in the design without creating a busy look. Because porches are open structures, the installation of an open apron like this seems right.

Right fit. An addition done in good taste is usually one where the size of new construction is determined by the dimensions of the existing house. A tiny entry porch here would have looked peculiar, and anything larger might have dwarfed the house.

Emotion. This porch project taps into a deep well of nostalgic American emotions. Isn't this a place for apple pie and lazy late-evening conversations? Your project doesn't have to appeal

▲ *Pine flooring was left unfinished so attention would be drawn toward the porch's painted beadboard ceiling. The extra effort spent in finishing the ceiling gives the whole project the snap of a starched collar.*

to the past. Whether yours is a sophisticated statement in marble or an expression of craftsmanship in oak, the particular style is not as important as the clarity of your design.

Top 10 Ways to Make a Good Impression

Here's the inside track to a good impression on those who drop by the house:

■ Be sure that exterior lights lead guests safely up the walkway.

■ Go out and ring your doorbell. Can your guests tell if you hear it inside? Is it pleasant-sounding? Visitors feel awkward if they fear no one on the inside knows they are there.

■ Choose friendly colors—perhaps a red door, a yellow entry accent wall, or a bright area rug—to warmly welcome guests.

■ Create a relaxed entry area for hellos and goodbyes. Buy or build in a display cabinet here to show off treasured items. If space is tight, hang a framed mirror above a slim shelf, or turn walls into a mini art gallery.

■ Include a closet or a country-style peg rack.

In cold climates, add a bench or a chair to make it easy for guests to remove their boots.

■ Instead of a single ceiling fixture, consider recessed can lights or a strip of track lights, which can be adjusted both to light the floor and highlight wall-hung artwork.

■ Use flooring of ceramic tile, brick, stone, or wood-look laminate so guests won't worry about tracked-in dirt or dripping umbrellas.

■ Design walls so your entry offers guests an intriguing glimpse of adjacent living spaces.

■ If you're building a new living room or great-room, position walls, fireplaces, and windows so that seating pieces can be grouped for easy conversation.

■ Wire an extra set of stereo speakers into your entry walls to greet guests with music.

Keep Everything on File

The day you sit down to sketch your addition or to meet with an architect, you should already have a good idea of your architectural style, the room decor you want, and where you will find the objects to fill the space. If you've prepared properly, it will all be in a notebook.

The chances of your project meeting or exceeding your dreams can be greatly increased by putting together a resource scrapbook well in advance of commencing construction. Some people have spent years piecing together the pictures, brochures, and notes that eventually become a road map defining the way for the project.

Within loose-leaf binders or accordion folders, you should gather information about:

■ Designs you like. Clip pictures from magazines that depict rooms you like or ideas you want to incorporate in your addition. It might be as simple as a wall color or as complex as a fireplace wall with built-in shelves and cabinets. This collection of photos will help you communicate your wishes during discussions with architects and designers. The right picture is worth a thousand words.

■ Product names and brochures. As you walk store aisles or visit design showrooms, write down the names of products you might like to incorporate in your project. Look for addresses and phone numbers on packages, too, because you may have trouble finding the same product months or years later when you want it. Also, pick up product brochures and send for catalogs.

■ Potential project team members. If possible, record the professional references you get from family and friends. Enter the names and phone numbers of architects, general contractors, or subcontractors in a notebook. Once the project is

▲ *Few turn-of-the-century homes would have been built with a sun-drenched sitting area such as this, and this home is no exception. The tall windows are part of a recent addition.*

under way, put together a separate ring binder in which you can keep track of the phone numbers and addresses of your project team members.

■ Schedules. Create schedules for work and for delivery of building materials. Keep these schedules handy and give all key players a copy.

■ Products. As the project progresses, be sure to keep all product information such as owner's manuals in a folder or notebook. You may not have to refer to it until months after the project is complete, but if your new heater goes out a year after installation, your notebook will save you from a frantic search for the installer's name.

Be sure to label all notebooks clearly so that other family members can identify them for the day something goes wrong and you're not home.

▲ *Floating a cooking island such as this into the center of a kitchen requires relocation of gas lines and venting ducts. Moving services is not too difficult, if access is available through a basement.*

▲ *Remodeling this kitchen required that gas lines be moved to provide fuel for the cooktop, plumbing be altered to accommodate the dishwasher and sink, and air-conditioning ducts be extended above the room.*

Heating and air-conditioning (HVAC).

Maintaining the comfort level of your addition requires adequate heating and cooling. It's wise to bring in professionals to determine if your equipment can condition the extra space built onto the house or if you will need additional equipment. If you have to purchase new equipment, here are choices you will face:

■ The efficiency of gas heaters today can reach 95 percent, which means almost all of the fuel is being transformed into heat. But the best units are also the most costly. If you live in cold coun-try where your heater runs through the whole winter, the fuel savings you'll achieve with a super-high-efficiency model may pay back the initial costs in a couple of years. But those living in warmer climates may find an 85 percent efficiency rating perfectly adequate.

■ When you add an average-size room, it can probably be tied to your home's existing ductwork and HVAC system. Window units will cool the room, but they are noisier, block out light, and are less appealing to potential buyers if you ever resell. If you are building a major addition, it

➤ *Gas fireplaces, such as the one in this keeping room, are easy to install because direct-vent chimneys are made with thin pipes rather than masonry. Brick is still often used, but only as a design element.*

➤ *Even brick facades are opening up these days. This line of 12-over-12 windows makes the keeping-room kitchen the bright spot of the house each day.*

may also be worthwhile shifting over to a ground-source heat-pump system for cooling and heating for your entire house. In moderate temperature zones, installation accounts for most of the cost. Operation is very inexpensive.

■ When you are designing the addition, you and your architect must consider where any new ducting will be installed. Often, a hollow opening or "chase" is created to handle ductwork. Creating a chase that is integral to the design of the addition and yet is virtually undetectable is one of the creative challenges of designing your addition.

■ A whole-house air-cleaning system that mounts at your heating and cooling unit is an increasingly popular investment. These systems use an electronic filter that removes particulates such as dust, pollen, and molds from the circulated air of your home. These systems can provide a healthier, cleaner indoor environment.

Specialty wiring. If you are thinking of including state-of-the-art electronics in your addition, such as a home theater, sophisticated sound system, security system, or telephone lines for your computer, be sure to include this possibility in your plan and budget. While new walls are open is an excellent, cost-effective time to provide the specialty wiring your lifestyle may require.

Safety First

As you protect your home against fire, burglary, and other misfortune, don't forget to guard against electrical surges.

All that expensive electronic gear in your home is at risk if the power surges because of lightning strikes or power company glitches. Standard 220-volt circuits can suddenly jump to 10,000 volts. When these spikes occur, microprocessors instantly fry inside your big-screen TV, desktop computer, sound equipment, and all those tiny computers managing appliances, lights, and other household functions.

Surge protectors are simple devices that stop excess electricity before it reaches your equipment. Anti-surge devices can be built into electronic systems during construction, or plugged in later.

Building a Healthy Home

Building an addition is an opportunity to include environmentally friendly designs and products that may even help you save money, especially with heating and cooling costs. Many companies offer products that are engineered for efficiency

▲ Polished granite was a stylish choice for the countertops in this kitchen. This stone comes with minimal environmental cost because it was locally quarried and is completely inert.

and have been designed to be compatible with different climates around the country.

■ Building materials. Generally, local materials are easier on the environment than those transported from a great distance. For example, granite quarried in your state will certainly require less fuel to deliver to your site than stone cut halfway around the world. Smaller companies that market locally can usually pass these kinds of savings on to consumers. Use only water-based finishes because they release few toxic gases into the air. Look for wood species, such as pine, that are plentiful and grown in managed forests.

■ Windows and appliances. Read energy tags when you shop for these important items. Look for windows that have double-pane, low-emissivity glass that will stop the transmission of heat. Efficient appliances are a must, too. Compare energy and water consumption between models before you buy.

■ Solar energy. Passive solar energy is free energy, so take advantage of it. Position the addition on your property so you can put in a wall of south-facing windows and enjoy a warm interior during winter.

▼ The greenhouse was added and the kitchen remodeled during construction. Plants scrub the air clean naturally for a healthy home.

➤ *One wall of the greenhouse (right and below) was angled to follow space for an existing driveway. Double-hung upper windows open for ventilation.*

■ Insulation. Insulate walls fully with an environmentally safe material, such as cellulose insulation made from recycled newspapers. When you're opening up your house for construction, it's a good time to inspect all air ducts for insulation and leaks. Up to 20 percent of the air you pay to heat leaks out of delivery ducts.

■ Natural cooling. Why pay utility companies for comfortable air, when shade trees will provide the same at no cost? Trees won't necessarily negate the need for a cooling system, but a shield of greenery will slow the assault of sunshine on your roof and walls.

■ Recycling center. If you are remodeling the kitchen, include a recycling center on the garage side of the room or in a utility room.

■ A good airing out. When construction is complete, you may have new countertops, carpets, tiles, and other materials containing glues, resins, and finishes that give off a variety of gases. Before moving in, ventilate the house for a couple of days, if possible. Odors disappear quickly if you help them along with a fan.

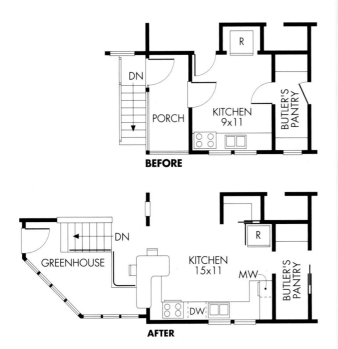

Experts' Insight

One of the best air filters you'll ever have may already be growing around your house, say NASA space scientists. Plants are nature's way of removing pollutants. Here are some of the more effective air cleaners:

■ Spider plants and golden pothos gobble up formaldehyde released by materials such as particleboard, insulation, and flooring.

■ Flowering plants, such as daisies, lilies, and chrysanthemums, are recommended for removing common household chemicals emitted from dry-cleaned clothing, varnishes, lacquers, and adhesives.

■ English ivy helps filter out benzine, a carcinogen found in tobacco smoke.

There's little danger that you will overstock a room with plants. Place at least one plant for each 100 square feet of interior space that needs continual cleaning.

Interior Changes

▲ Ceilings pressed down low throughout the house before this family room was added. Vaulted ceilings and bold windows give the home personality.

◄ The front facade of this uninspiring 1940s house was perked up with a 700-square-foot addition. Both new and old windows have black shutters.

Creative visualization is an important part of determining how your addition will be shaped and styled. The trick is, you have to see something that's not there. For instance, if your present home has standard eight-foot ceilings, you might want to imagine the addition with ceilings that soar. Or, if your kitchen is dull and outdated, you'll need to envision it with new colors and sparkling surfaces.

Today, there are many computer programs available that help homeowners with creative visualization. Many of these programs allow you to "build" a new floor plan for your house, then "tour" the results in a three-dimensional rendering that can be rotated and viewed from various angles. If you have access to a home computer, such a program can be a valuable tool to help you get the results you want. Sophisticated architectural programs can cost hundreds of dollars, but you can purchase an effective one for $50 or less.

As you visualize your new addition, keep these ideas in mind:

■ Light is particularly important when adding a kitchen. Look for ways to add windows or drop in skylights, so that the kitchen comes alive at morning light. If the position of the skylights will occasionally allow in too much sunshine, order units with motorized blinds so you can shut out midday light at the flip of a switch.

■ A single strong design element can create a signature for your home. Try scouting architectural salvage yards for an antique mantel or a one-of-a-kind entry hall chandelier that invests your home with your personality.

■ An addition provides an opportunity to make a new space for hobbies or personal interests that for too long have been cramped into other spaces. If the desk in your bedroom is overflowing with craft materials because you have nowhere else to store them, maybe the room addition could include a craft center. Or consider creating a sewing room, a gift-wrapping station, or a place to make flower arrangements.

■ Think of features that will make maintenance of the home easier. This could be a new master bathroom with slick, water-shedding surfaces. The existing bath may be a swamp of grime. In the new bathroom, design a walk-in shower that needs no door or curtain. Install solid-surface material countertops that withstand years of punishment and a one-piece toilet that can be cleaned without the need for a bucket brigade.

■ There's no need to live with a laundry room that leaves you feeling dingy. Even in homes with terrific living spaces, the laundry is sometimes laid out as an inconvenient afterthought. This could be the time to build an all-new laundry with ample room to handle this necessary chore.

Experts' Insight

You may not have given any thought to universal design—you may not even be familiar with the term. Universal design means rooms are created with accessibility for those with handicaps. There are no barriers or encumbrances that might pose difficulties to the free movement of those who are physically challenged. This approach to design is common in public buildings, particularly since the passage of the Americans with Disabilities Act. It's a philosophy that can fit homes, too.

If the design is a good one, few will even take notice. It's a simple matter of leaving paths and doorways wide enough for wheelchairs; keeping floor heights the same level so there is no need for thresholds that can stop wheels or cause stumbling; selecting easy-open latches instead of knobs for door handles; putting wheelchair wells beneath bathroom sinks; and choosing large paddle handles for faucets instead of smaller knobs. Most of these and similar choices are aesthetically appealing and easy to install; they are simply different than most of us are used to.

An aging population is demanding easier-to-use products from designers, but it's making life better for everyone. Plumbing manufacturers have created shower grab bars that are stylish and helpful, cabinet companies have come up with drawers that glide effortlessly, and catalogs offer dozens of other helpful products that are only a phone call away.

An Improved Floor Plan

Remodelers can learn from the experience of the couple who bought this 100-year-old Queen Anne-style Victorian house for love of its quaint architectural detailing—but not its kitchen.

Not long after moving in, they began updating the floor plan to include a modern kitchen with high-pitched ceilings and a relaxed attitude. They did most of the work themselves, which saved money but took nearly a year to complete.

To gain square footage, they annexed an unheated back porch. This new arrangement also opened views to the west and south, lighting up the room. A new, smaller entry still offers plenty of space for coats and a recycling center.

Rearranging space was easy, compared with raising the ceiling. To raise the ceiling, a new roof section was built several feet above the old. After this was in place, the old ceiling and roof were torn away from the inside to make way for new ceiling drywall.

The new arrangement not only accesses the former mudroom's space and views, but it also makes room for a wet bar and an ample cooking island with counter seating. By flanking a window with a built-in rolltop desk and a display cabinet, the owners even made space for a charming window seat.

▲ *For visual variety and cost savings, the owners splurged on an island topped with green granite but used more affordable plastic laminate on other countertops.*

➤ *The floor plans reveal different ways of living. In the past, muddy feet seemed to be a big deal. Now, it's more important that the cook be included in family life.*

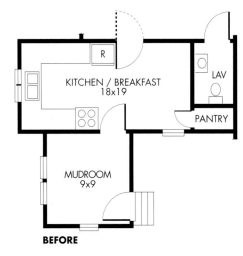

BEFORE

AFTER

▲ *Looking for ways to save on their remodeling, the homeowners found the hanging lamp and the dining room chairs at garage sales. A window seat behind the table provides a relaxing view.*

Building with Style

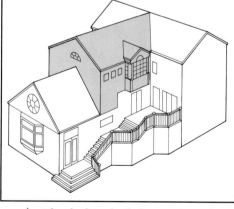

The darker shaded area shows how the addition straddles two levels of roof on the original house.

▲ *Although the master bathroom is only 6 feet wide, there's more than enough room because it is 20 feet long.*

▲ *By including a small bump-out in the plans for the addition, this handsome retreat bay was created.*

Style isn't a neutral word. It takes a certain amount of courage—and usually the help of a talented architect or designer—to create a new addition that is spirited and filled with character. Often the best, most satisfying results come from a process of designing and redesigning, and from the uncompromising attitude of homeowners who refuse to settle for anything less than great design. Happily, excellent design doesn't necessarily mean a costly, complicated project.

The family that created the second-story addition shown on these pages knew what they were doing. The 400-square-foot addition that now sits atop their Colonial-style home in Maryland neatly straddles an existing one-story section of their house. The exterior elements connect so smoothly that the structure seems of one piece in color, texture, and style. Inside, imaginative window designs and high ceilings create drama and interest. Trim details echo the home's traditional architecture.

The homeowners attribute the success of this project to a design phase that finalized many details, including the interior design. In fact, any good addition and remodeling should start with a complete understanding of how you want the interiors to look and function. What types of furniture pieces will you use and how might they be arranged? In too many cases, walls are designed and features such as fireplaces built in before the owners realize that the resulting space makes room arranging difficult. To smooth your way, consider hiring an interior designer to help see you through all the way to the finished—and furnished—interiors.

To be sure that you and your design team are on the same wavelength, share magazine clippings and take time to browse shops and model homes together. Along the way, make sure everyone is clear about their design responsibilities and that you have the final say-so on all decisions.

▲ *The second-story master suite addition and outdoor stairs bridge the two older parts of the home. A storage area was also built under the deck and enclosed with wooden lattice panels.*

Case History

When homeowner Bruce Carlyle wanted to fashion the perfect deck overlooking Long Island Sound, he enlisted the skills of an architect, a landscape architect, an interior designer, and a specialty painter.

"Everyone brings different talents to a project and sees something that no one else sees. I just sit in the middle and pick out the best of all the ideas," Bruce says.

The architect shaped the basic design.

The landscape architect fashioned a row of hedges along the front of the deck that adds color and acts as a privacy screen.

The interior designer found a brass shower made in the 1920s that now awaits Bruce when he rushes in from a splash in the ocean.

The painter, whose usual assignment is dining room murals, adorned the deck with painted naval caps and anchors.

The Eyes of the House

▲ *Tall casement windows over this sink area overlook a back porch. If it gets a little steamy at this clean-up center, the windows can be pushed open. A lineup of jewel-like blue bottles adds a splash of color.*

Windows are one of the most important elements of house design. Today's window manufacturers offer a variety of shapes, colors, and technologies suited to many kinds of installations and climates. As you develop your plans, some knowledge of window types and terms will help you achieve your design goals. You can install vinyl-clad windows and never paint again, order tip-out windows so outside surfaces are almost as easy to clean as inside, and purchase glass coated with finishes to keep heat where you want it so window walls add to the comfort of a room.

Double-pane (insulated). This is the industry standard. Each window is made with two identically sized sheets of glass separated a quarter-inch or so to create a thin air pocket. This air break significantly slows the passage of heat. Even more effective (and costly) are triple-pane windows.

Gas-filled. The air chamber between windows may be filled with argon or some other gas that is heavier than air and effectively slows heat.

Low-emissivity (low-E). This is a thin metallic coating that is bonded to the glass. You can see through it, but heat will be reflected off of it.

Thermal breaks. These are chambers or barriers built into frames that also serve to stop the transmission of heat. While they are an important feature for wood and vinyl windows, they are critical to the performance of an aluminum frame because metal conducts heat in abundance. High-tech plastic breaks are built into aluminum frames to act as buffers between exterior metal surfaces and those on the interior.

As you shop for windows, compare both the R-values and U-values on different products. These are measurements of how effectively windows resist or allow heat gain. The better the window, the higher the R-values and lower the U-values.

There are good windows made in wood, vinyl, and aluminum frames. Look closely at each type of window before deciding which is right for you. Wood offers wonderful aesthetics in a variety of styles, vinyl is durable and easy to maintain, and aluminum performs well in warmer climates and fits most budgets.

➤ *High-rise windows wrap around two sides of a roomy kitchen, drawing sun deep into the work area. Double-hung lower units were chosen so they could be opened for fresh air from the garden.*

Design Checklists

As you meet with architects, designers, government officials, subcontractors, and others, be prepared to answer the questions below. Those you work with will certainly come up with more questions, but knowing these answers will save time as you begin planning with professionals.

Your House and Its Occupants

■ Style of your house?

■ Year it was built?

■ Size in square feet?

■ Overall dimensions?

■ Orientation of the house: North? South? East? West?

■ General type of construction: Brick? Wood frame? Other?

■ Type of foundation?

■ Type of windows?

■ Type of roofing material?

■ Type of siding?

■ Is there a basement?

■ How many people live in the house? Will that be changing in the foreseeable future?

■ Do you entertain often? Does the present setup of the house accommodate your entertaining requirements?

■ Are the sizes of public spaces adequate?

■ Do you desire more quiet and privacy?

Building the Addition

■ What type of addition do you want?

■ To what degree do you expect this to be a do-it-yourself project?

■ Who will do design work?

■ Who will construct the project?

■ Who will obtain permits?

■ What are the set-back restrictions of your lot?

■ Does your home fall within any other special restrictions, such as those of a historic district or a covenant community?

■ Will you supply any of the materials?

■ What is the timetable for the project?

■ What is the overall budget?

■ Is the project being financed by a bank or lending institution? Or is it being paid for from savings or some other way?

Kitchen Additions

■ Who will design the kitchen? A Certified Kitchen Designer? The architect? Another designer or yourself?

■ What style will cabinetry be?

■ What cabinet company will you use?

■ Will the plumbing wall be moved?

■ Are you adding appliances to the kitchen that will need 220-volt electric service or any other special lines?

■ Will any walls be removed?

■ Do you want additional windows or skylights?

■ Are you hiring a lighting designer?

■ Do you want additional electric outlets?

Bathroom Additions

■ Will the locations of any fixtures or the shower change?

■ Do you want separate shower and tub?

■ Are you adding a jetted tub?

■ Does your home need new water or drain pipes?

■ Do you need more space for the bathroom?

■ Do you want additional electric outlets?

■ Is the location of the main bathroom convenient to the master bedroom and closets?

■ What surface materials do you want in the bathroom? Ceramic tile? Vinyl?

Living Room or Family Room Additions

■ Do you want the new room to open onto other rooms?

■ Will there be exterior doors? Should they be fully or partially glazed?

■ Are you adding a window wall?

■ Are you adding a gas fireplace? Will you build a hearth area with a mantel?

■ What kind of floors do you want? Carpet? Wood and rugs?

General Design Questions

■ What are your favorite colors?

■ Does the household gather for meals? What is the breakfast routine? What about dinner?

■ Do you have swatches of fabric, paint color chips, or pieces of wallpaper that capture the look you desire? Is there a place in your present home to display your collections? What do you collect?

Creating an Exterior

Get out your pencils once again as you create exterior renderings of your house as it is and as you want it to be.

In one of the boxes provided here—or on separate graph paper or on a computer—draw a simple picture of your house, showing it from the angle (or angles) that will be affected by the addition. You'll probably have to make more than one drawing. Note locations of windows, doors, and other exterior features, and keep the drawing in scale to the best of your ability. Also, draw the roof as if you were looking straight down on it from high above.

After the present exterior is down on paper, start drawing the exterior as it might look with the addition.

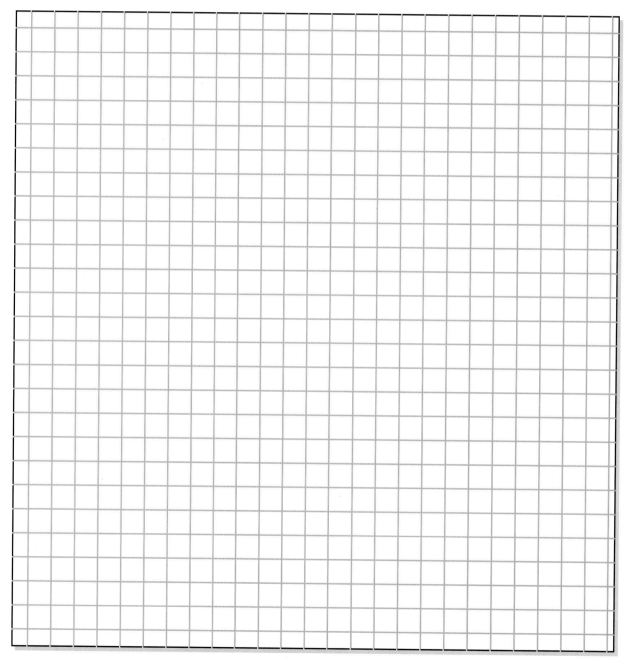

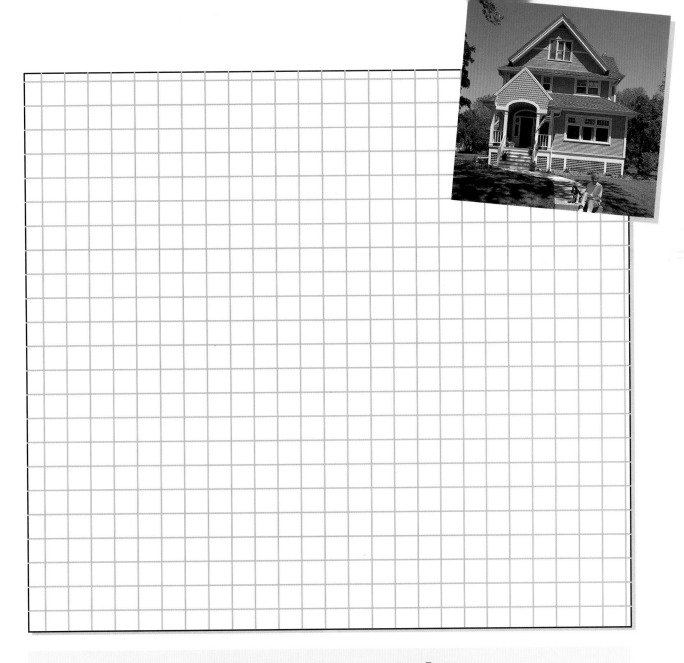

Experts' Insight

Most of us are honest enough to admit we are a little embarrassed by the way we draw. Wouldn't you rather clap erasers than show your artwork to an architect or designer? Fortunately, your personal computer can help.

Software companies recognize that building additions has become the new national pastime, so they are continually marketing more and ever-better programs that will help you design your addition. With the best of these programs, you can design floor plans, draw exterior renderings, and move rapidly through an array of color-coded, 3-D changes. These programs will help you get the most design in the least amount of time.

But don't be fooled into thinking that these powerful tools will replace the need for outside design consultants. Just because a machine can help you define your options, doesn't mean it is particularly skilled at helping you make the right decision. That's why you pay for experienced experts.

Drawing It Up

You're ready to move beyond design discussions and solidify your ideas—it's time to draw up blueprints.

The plans for your addition are now ready to become a series of construction documents outlining every detail—from the thickness of wall insulation to the silhouette of crown molding. Finalizing your plans is a time of excitement and even a little anxiety.

In this phase you will make the last adjustments to the floor plan, prepare a site plan, and begin creating blueprints. You'll need a clear head and an eye for detail as you repeatedly go over the evolving plans. This is when you want to catch small mistakes and make those minor adjustments that will ensure your addition fulfills your dreams.

Be prepared for a lot of give and take with designers and architects as you hammer out a seemingly endless list of specifics. If you have a fax machine, keep it loaded with paper so you can keep current with the latest revisions. If you're someone who only transacts business face-to-face, keep the car filled with gas. The whole project is shifting into high gear.

At this stage, you will evaluate what kind of design and drawing help you may need. Although working with an architect is ideal, it doesn't fit into everyone's budget. But even if your funds are tight, consider paying an architect for a design consultation. You can control the costs by paying by the hour and setting a limit on the number of hours you want the architect to spend on your project.

As you look into design assistance, you'll also want to consider the pros and cons of computer-aided design (CAD) programs. They can help you plan and visualize your project, but they might put the brakes on your own creativity. For example, kitchens designed on such systems function well, yet they often have a sameness about them because of the limitations of the programs' built-in design choices.

➤ *Before remodeling, the exterior of this house was composed mainly of brick. Even though the extensive wing addition was faced with stucco and stone materials, it blends smoothly with the original. To help unify the structure, brick salvaged during the demolition was used to trim the addition.*

Evolution of a Floor Plan

Although the addition to the home shown on these pages was modest—only a total of 168 square feet was added—the results were a big improvement in livability. The key to the success of this project was the homeowners' tireless search for just the right architect. They interviewed seven different design professionals before deciding on one who they believed would be able to translate their vision to reality.

Making this addition work was an important goal. The homeowners had lived in this house for 20 years, and after their children had grown, they considered moving to a bigger house. But a comparable home would have cost many times more than they wanted to spend. They decided to stay put and make a more sensible investment in an addition instead.

The new floor plan allowed the breakfast room and cooking areas to become part of the

▲ *A simple addition combined with the removal of walls turned an ordinary 1960s family room into a cheery, light-filled space with a casual, open floor plan.*

▼ *Building an addition to extend the family room was only part of the change. Walls separating the kitchen, breakfast room, and family room area were removed to create one unified space.*

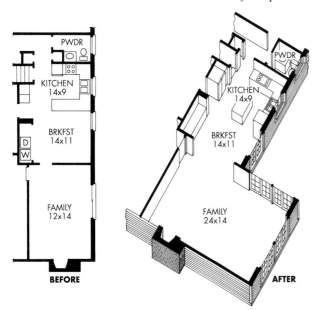

Money $ Saver

Trying to spare your wallet can prove an expensive strategy for do-it-yourselfers. Consider new kitchen cabinets.

Excellent cabinets from first-rate companies are now available at home centers around the country. Properly ordered and installed on perfectly plumb walls, these can be a great buy for homeowners.

But what if your walls aren't plumb? Or you order the cabinets before the walls are completely built—and walls wind up 2 inches off square? What if the sink falls 4 inches away from the spot where the plan showed it would go? Or what if you simply measured wrong?

Accurate field measurements after drywall is up are a must. Put a level on the walls and floors to see that everything is square. Compare outlets against the plans. Check and recheck everything before ordering.

▲ *The original family room took on old-world character with plank wood floors and carefully chosen antique accents. The ceiling was raised to a height of 14 feet and the vaulted ceiling's pine beams were left uncovered to give the room a casual touch. Pine window and door moldings carry out the vintage look.*

family room and permitted an easier and more casual exchange between family and guests. Whoever's cooking now has a clear line of sight from the kitchen island through the breakfast area to the spacious family room beyond. This type of reconfiguring of interior spaces takes into account certain value considerations such as the ability to converse easily and a feeling of togetherness. As you approach your own remodeling, look for similar ways to make the most of your floor plan alterations. If this small addition can pay such returns on its investment, so can yours.

Getting the Site Right

An important part of committing your ideas to final plans is adjusting your addition to its site. Although this consideration is more appropriate for larger additions, such as wings, any addition can benefit from considering views and solar gain from direct sunlight.

Along with project blueprints that detail house construction, you should draw up a site plan showing the present location of trees, hills, and other landscape features. Note locations of streets, power lines, and sewers. It will make planning easier if you include the direction of the morning, midday, and evening sun at various times of the year. Each of these details may affect the way you build your addition.

Design your addition so it makes the most of existing trees, sloping hills, and other landscape features. You may put in a window to frame the perfect view of an old oak tree, decide to add a walk-out basement to take advantage of a sloped lot, or add a second floor that takes inspiration from surrounding mountains.

During construction, protect existing plants and trees with small fences and signs. If large trucks or tractors will be running over areas where tree roots are growing, put down sheets of plywood to cushion their impact as much as possible. Trees can be killed if roots are crushed.

You may also want to work with a landscape designer to develop a plan for improving the lot after construction is complete. The site will suffer damage as workers and heavy equipment come and go, so you should plant trees, grass, and flowers after they leave.

Experts' Insight

As you begin to move from planning to the construction phase, heed the advice of smart do-it-yourselfers who know they can rent special tools to make jobs quicker and easier.

If you encounter difficulty during construction, see if the following tools are locally available. Generally, the more expensive the retail price of a tool, the more you will save if you can rent it.

■ Nail guns. Take some of the tedium out of framing additions and laying subfloors by using a nail gun. Shooting nails is much easier on arms than hammering. Some models are electric, but others are pneumatic, so you may need to rent an air compressor, too. If you do, the compressor can power other tools, such as painting equipment.

■ Table saws. This tool is indispensible if you are adding entire rooms and cutting a lot of plywood sheeting in the process.

■ Power post-hole diggers. It will take two people to heft a power auger for digging holes, but they can bore a hole in most soils in a matter of seconds. Consider this tool if you need to dig many holes for fencing or building an extensive deck.

■ Cement mixers. For installation of driveways, call in cement trucks that deliver concrete by the yard. If you are using only small amounts of cement, mix it yourself with an electric power mixer.

■ Small tractors. If you are leveling a lot, scraping the ground smooth with a rental tractor will cost much less than hiring a heavy equipment operator.

■ Space heater. If your project gets off schedule and you find yourself working in an unheated room in winter, rent a space heater to keep comfortable. Ask the rental agent to size the heater to your room.

■ Power painting equipment. Professionals avoid painting by hand because it is a boring, time-consuming task. Follow their lead and rent power equipment for the job.

▲ *The original structure (the section with the porch) was lifted two feet so the foundation could be rebuilt. Then the wing was added (to the right). All this work was done while preserving as many trees as possible.*

From Plan to Blueprint

The last step in finalizing your plan is preparing a set of blueprints. The blueprints tell the builder and the subcontractors exactly how the addition will be constructed.

▲ *When homeowners decided to add a second story to their small, single-level ranch, imaginative planning was the key to success. A tiny hallway became the perfect place to tuck the stairs to the new upper story.*

Unless you have experience creating blueprints, you will need an architect, a draftsman, or your design/builder team to prepare blueprints for your project. Plans that you have prepared yourself or that were drawn by a designer other than an architect will need to be certified by a structural engineer before you will be issued a building permit. In some cases, you may be working from stock plans that came from a plan publisher or were supplied by a design company.

Regardless of a plan's origin, you will need several copies (at least eight) of the master set because many people involved with the project will need to review copies. These might include:
■ Your city or county building agency. They may request two or more copies, depending on their requirements. Copies may be requested for a planning commission, a structural or mechanical engineer, an environmental resources agency, a historic district board, or others. Each agency will inspect the blueprints and approve the project after you request a building permit.
■ The general contractor. Whoever is overseeing the job requires two sets of blueprints.
■ Special designers. Copies may be requested by the interior designer, kitchen designer, lighting designer, and others.
■ Yourself. If you are running the job yourself, keep two copies. One can be a working copy—it can be taken apart and notes can be scribbled on it. But keep a clean copy locked away as a backup. You may need it and it should stay with the house if you ever sell it.

If your home will be significantly altered by the addition, extra drawings sometimes help negotiations with various subcontractors and suppliers. If there are details that are particularly important, be sure to enlarge that section of the plan or have your draftsman produce detailed drawings so that specifications are easy to read and understand.

It's essential that you study the blueprints yourself to make sure all you've asked for is specified on paper. Naturally, it is much easier to request changes to the blueprints than ask for alterations to the addition once it has been built. Blueprints should include lists showing the dimensions of doors and windows, locations of light fixtures, wall switches, and electrical outlets, and the placement of heating vents and air returns. All details of construction will be shown in blueprint symbols. If you don't know what a symbol means, ask your architect or designer for an explanation.

▲ *This kitchen is filled with details that had to be specified on the blueprints, including the use of pine planks for the ceiling, the locations of the two sinks, the positions of recessed and decorative lighting, and the shape and size of the arched window at the main cleanup area.*

PHASE 5: CONSTRUCTION ZONE

Managing Your Project

To help your project run smoothly, stay organized and keep track of finances.

The actual start of the construction phase is an exciting and hectic time, with saws buzzing and hammers pounding out their rhythms. It may be that your normal domestic routines will be disrupted, but achieving your final goal will soon make all the noise and dust worthwhile.

As the construction begins and work progresses, there is still much for you to do. You'll need to take time on a regular basis to visit with your general contractor or your various subcontractors to make sure that materials arrive on time and that the work is on schedule. Even if your addition was planned down to the smallest detail, there will still probably be decisions to make that only you, as homeowner, should make.

You'll also want to monitor expenses so that you can be assured your project remains on budget. All this requires that you keep paperwork and schedules organized. Also, a basic knowledge of the construction process will help you do what you can to keep everything running smoothly.

➤ *The addition of this vinyl bay window raised the value of a Colonial-style home by about $10,000. The investment? About $2,100 for the window and $1,725 for roofing, flashing, framing, and other installation materials and expenses. The job took only a weekend because the bay replaced a window of similar size.*

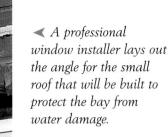
◄ A professional window installer lays out the angle for the small roof that will be built to protect the bay from water damage.

▼ A workman uses a high-speed cutter to etch a thin groove into the brick. This creates a seat for copper flashing that provides a seal along the top of the bay's roof. Metal flashing is always needed at all roof joints to protect wood framing and plywood underlayment from getting wet and rotting.

Teamwork and Paperwork

If you are hiring a general contractor, the agreement you put on paper will define that relationship and play an important part in determining whether the building goes well or not. You must understand every clause within the contract, so discuss it with an attorney if you have questions. Look for these elements within the contract:

■ A general description of the work and the location where it will be performed.

■ The price of the work and a breakdown of payments. Breaking the price into three, four, or more payments will help you maintain leverage in case there are disagreements about the work. Some contractors will ask for a down payment up front to cover the cost of materials. Pay no more than necessary for this, generally about 25–30 percent. For major jobs, it's best to stagger material payments so they are made about the same time as the goods are needed. There's no need to pay for cabinets now if they won't be ordered for three months, for instance.

■ List the responsibilities of the owner, including any materials that you will supply or parts of the job that you will handle (such as daily site clean-up or interior painting). Note who will obtain permits and specifics about insurance covering the job site.

■ List the responsibilities of the contractor, including materials they will supply and subcontractors they will coordinate and supervise.

■ A timetable should fix a starting date, set milestone dates along the way that mark the project's progress, and a completion date.

■ Accompanying the contract will be blueprints, shop drawings, and any other documents that impact design and construction. They become part of the contract.

■ There may also be penalties for failures to perform. These are built into agreements to make sure jobs run on time and on budget. It's also effective to put small incentives in contracts for jobs done above expectations. For instance, add a $300 end-of-job bonus to encourage workers to keep a building site clean.

Experts' Insight

Too many building projects end with contractors and homeowners threatening lawsuits over disagreements. If you keep precise, written change orders current throughout the course of the project, you probably won't have to visit a courtroom.

Whenever you decide to make a change to the blueprint or agreed-upon building plan, take a moment to write a description of the change. It should include the date, describe the change, and be initialed by both the homeowner and contractor.

The key element is cost. Note any additional expense that the alteration requires. This may include costs of tearing out the existing work and adding in whatever new element you have ordered.

▲ *The shaded area indicates how the long, narrow second story was added to this older home. The original budget was $30,000, but the price of the finished addition soared to almost $60,000.*

▲ *A contemporary, open-grid front facade put sensational style in what had been a typically small turn-of-the-century home in Seattle.*

➤ *The architecture of the home retains some of its Victorian roots, but it has been updated with new siding and windows.*

A Question of Money

▲ *Building a sunroom such as this requires you gather price quotes from makers of windows, columns, gutters, roofing, flooring, and other materials.*

Money $ Saver

Here are 10 ways to save you money when building an addition:
- Purchase materials yourself.
- Pay for the project as you go.
- Hire professionals for design work.
- Hire a general contractor to direct your building project.
- Limit do-it-yourself work to those jobs that you have some experience doing.
- Inspect the job at the end of each work day to minimize unwanted surprises.
- Make changes when the project is in the design phase, not the building phase.
- Once the plan is set, stick to it.
- Design to please yourself, not some unknown buyer you may not meet for years to come.
- Remember the lesson of Fred Astaire: Simplicity is the partner of elegance.

Financing your addition is one of the more critical issues you'll face. If you can pay for your project from your savings, you'll avoid finance charges. However, a substantial addition project usually requires that the homeowner borrow money from a lending institution. In that case, you may finance the effort with credit cards or other payment terms, put the tab on a personal loan, take out a second mortgage based on the equity you have in your home, refinance and increase the size of your present mortgage, borrow against insurance, or qualify for a federal remodeling program. Here are some advantages and disadvantages of each:

- Credit cards or other credit terms. Work charged to your card or paid to an installation company in monthly payments stretches out the cost. But watch out for high interest, which can build a big price into a small addition.
- Personal loans. If a bump-out can be added for under $5,000, you may get a reasonably low-interest loan through a credit union or other small lending company.
- Second mortgage. Interest on these loans can be very attractive, and you are usually allowed to borrow up to 100 percent of the equity on your home. Interest paid on money for home improvements is presently deductible on income taxes, too, which makes this a good alternative.
- Refinancing. Instead of a second mortgage, you might want to take out a new loan that is large enough to pay off your existing house loan and also includes monies to pay for your addition. This strategy can work if the new interest rate is significantly lower than that of your original loan. Don't forget to calculate loan-transfer fees into the equation, however. Interest on these loans is tax deductible, too.
- Insurance loans. Some insurance policies allow the borrower to take out loans.
- Federal programs. These types of loans are fairly rare, but the Housing and Urban Development Administration (HUD) still makes limited amounts of money available for those who are fixing up homes in blighted areas. There are also

▲ *Transom windows across the top of the sunroom's window walls are lined with antique bottles, adding brilliant color to this light space. When breezes blow, fresh air can be invited in by opening the windows.*

some funds available from both local and federal agencies for those improving homes in historic districts. Check with local housing authorities to see if you can qualify for any of this money.

If trying to save money is part of your financial strategy, consider doing some of the work yourself. You might even coordinate with your building contractor to take on areas of responsibility, such as installing trim or painting walls. Make sure your contracts specify your involvement, and that the contractor isn't responsible for the quality of your efforts.

Another strategy is to start stockpiling materials months or years before work begins on the addition. You may not be able to afford a whole bath-full of fixtures today, but could you afford just a tub? How about a new vanity next month? A pedestal sink the month after? This will spread out investment and allow you to track down the best deal on each item you buy. In addition to sale items, you have time to search out antique shops, factory closeouts, special catalog offerings, and items posted for sale through classified ads in your local newspaper.

The Construction Process

The construction of most addition projects begins with destruction. Whether you are pulling down, punching through, or tearing out, the first few days will be taken up with demolition and hauling away the rubble.

Once the mess is cleared, you must start at the bottom and work up. This usually means laying out a new foundation or setting footings. During this phase of the work, heavy equipment may be rumbling across your property, so take precautions to protect landscaping as described earlier.

Framing the walls and roof will take anywhere from a couple of days to a couple weeks, depending on the size of the job. As the outline of the room or rooms takes shape, keep your tape measure handy so you can check the work against blueprints. Measure window-frame sizes and make certain they are where you want them.

After framing is up, the exterior will be sheathed with plywood. While walls are still open to the inside, wiring, plumbing, heating-and-cooling ducts, and insulation are placed inside the wall cavities. These systems are followed by the installation of the windows and roof, as well as roofing materials and exterior siding. The addition is now fully "weathered in."

On the inside, the walls will be covered with a surfacing material, usually drywall. After drywall is completed, the room can be painted. Flooring is next. If you are putting down hardwood, make certain you have it on the job site at least a week ahead of time so it can acclimate to the humidity level where you live.

If you are building a kitchen, the cabinets are

Experts' Insight

Construction days will bring visits from your friendly building inspector. Here are the stages when you may need their signature:
- Completion of the foundation.
- Completion of framing.
- Following installation of roof system.
- When mechanicals are installed.
- Before walls are sealed.
- After all other interior work is done.

Your local building ordinances may require a Certificate of Occupancy. This certificate allows you to live in your addition. Check with your local planning commission to see if it is required.

▼ *This was an unassuming one-story house until additions pumped it up. The first floor doubled in size, and a second story and loft were added.*

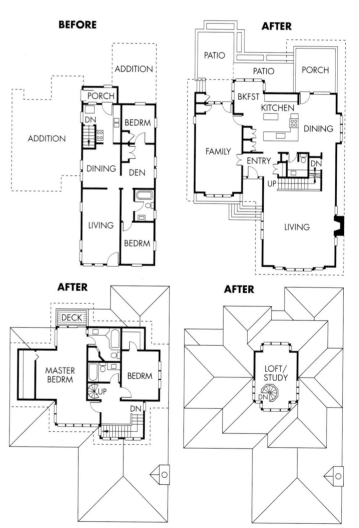

▲ *The new living room takes up almost as much space as the living room, a bedroom, a bathroom, and the dining room did in the home's original layout.*

now set in place. Countertops go down next, followed by plumbing fixtures and appliances.

Those putting in bathrooms will be setting tiles and putting in fixtures last, except the tub. Tubs usually go in following framing and are built right into the walls.

The final steps are trimming rooms with molding, hanging doors, installing any built-in furniture, and installing lamp fixtures. If you are carpeting rooms, it usually goes in last to protect it from paint or other damage.

▲ *Reconfiguring a simple one-story home as a spacious three-level showplace took four years. The homeowner, an architect, redesigned the house and served as general contractor. He subcontracted the foundation, plumbing, wiring, and mechanical work.*

Homework: 6-Month Schedule

Although the length and complexity of addition projects vary, the basic outline of the schedule is consistent. Use this six-month calendar to help you keep track of project progress:

First Month
Preliminary meeting with architect
or designer ....Date: _____
Second meeting with architect or
designer at the building site ....Date: _____

Second Month
Third meeting with architect or designer
for final review of plans ....Date: _____

Third Month
Break ground ....Date: _____
Order windows ....Date: _____
Order concrete...Date: _____
Order framing lumber ....Date: _____
Order roof trusses and shingles ....Date: _____
Order engineered wood ....Date: _____
Foundation work ....Started: _____Completed: _____
Framing..Started: _____Completed: _____
Order plumbing fixtures ....Date: _____
Order cabinets ....Date: _____

Fourth Month
Install roofing ....Started: _____Completed: _____
Install windows...Started: _____Completed: _____
Rough in plumbing,
   electrical, HVAC,
   insulation..Started: _____Completed: _____
Put up drywall ....Started: _____Completed: _____
Order countertops ....Date: _____
Order flooring ....Date: _____
Order doors and millwork ....Date: _____

Fifth Month
Paint exterior ....Started: _____Completed: _____
Paint interior ....Started: _____Completed: _____
Install flooring ....Started: _____Completed: _____
Install cabinets ....Started: _____Completed: _____
Install countertops ....Started: _____Completed: _____

Sixth Month
Install fixtures, electrical,
   doors, trim, and appliances ....Job Completed: _____

Before remodeling, the front door of this Wisconsin farmhouse led abruptly into the living room. The welcoming new entry porch (at left) leads into a separate vestibule (above and right) that greets guests with a homey display of books and collectibles. A convenient guest coat closet and new half-bath hide behind closed doors.

New Outlook

This page begins a tour of inspiring additions. Bring along your imagination and take home some fresh ideas.

The owners of a 1930s story-and-a-half Colonial first planned minor updating for their riverside home in Winnipeg, Manitoba, Canada. Perhaps they'd be ambitious and move a wall. But an architect helped them develop a much more elaborate plan that gave their home a sunny new disposition.

As originally built, the main house and a garage were separated by a breezeway. A two-story addition slipped right into that opening and invested new life into the entire house with an 18×21-foot sunroom. The spectacular new room brings in views from three directions.

This was a case where an addition helped solve an awkward problem. The project allowed simplification of the home's rear roofline, and it's never looked better.

The sunroom also created a natural courtyard where a brick patio was installed for lounging and outdoor dining.

The homeowners were thrilled with the results and say, "We knew we would never do this kind of project again, so we wanted it to be as perfect as possible."

▲ Custom-milled French windows crowned with a broad fanlight create a space with warmth and a great view toward trees and a river. Track lighting illuminates the night.

▼ *The shaded area of the home's exterior shows how the addition was placed between the existing house (on the left) and garage (on the right). The home's front entry was moved into the addition, where it was given more space.*

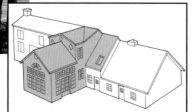

▲ *Sunroom windows weren't the only benefit of the addition. A skylight, a diamond window, and other windows were popped in, too.*

➤ *A new stairwell features a ziggurat motif, as do storage niches underneath and a custom-made glass-top coffee table. Windows in the stairwell also spread a little sunshine.*

Honeymoon Suite

It didn't take long for a newlywed couple to realize their Santa Fe-style home could accommodate them but not all their wardrobe. So four months after moving into this 1,600-square-foot house, they added a 900-square-foot master bedroom suite overlooking a golf course.

The addition includes a cathedral-ceiling master bedroom and a master bath with an oversized whirlpool tub for two. A spacious walk-in closet was located a few steps away from the bedroom

▲ *The backyard is now sheltered by the addition. The architect took care to ensure that the roof pitch and other exterior details all matched.*

▼ *Pedestal sinks are handsome but offer no counter space. Here, a sliver of bumped-out wall space contains bins for towels below and a ledge for toiletries on top.*

▲ *Tiled shelves at a variety of levels around the whirlpool tub make plenty of display area for plants and collectibles. Hidden from view is an access panel for the whirlpool's motor. Don't overlook this important item when designing your own bathroom.*

▲ *To give walls character, decorative recesses were built in next to windows.*

➤ *The shaded area shows the arrangement of the master suite addition. A slight bump-out along one bedroom wall created space for three windows and a small sitting area.*

so either of the couple can get dressed quietly should the two be on different schedules. A single French door in the bedroom leads to a small terrace, a perfect spot for breakfast or brunch during the summer months.

The addition blends smoothly with the existing structure. Archways around the doors and windows look the same in the new and older sections of the house. Outside, red clay tiles tied the addition's roof into the existing one. After building was completed, the entire house was covered with fresh stucco to ensure a perfect match.

The ambience is just right. With the doors and windows open, this city house feels as if it has been set down in the country.

A Simple Solution

Maintaining the original romantic flavor of an aging home—without spending a fortune—could have been a difficult assignment for the owners of this stone gatehouse. But the simple sunroom addition they built shows how it can be done with standard glass sliding doors, some redwood lumber, and a bit of imagination.

Added to a turn-of-the-century Connecticut cottage, the light, airy room is basically a 17×13-foot box built with pine lumber and lined with sliding doors. Its charm is the result of exterior-mounted redwood trellises that create a transom-like arch at the top of the sliders. Viewed from inside, the exterior trelliswork creates a pleasing architectural detail and mimics the home's original diamond-pane windows.

The trellises are inexpensive and easy to build. As newly planted trumpet vines and clematis vines climb up and fill in the grid, the room will take on more detail and color. The sunroom becomes a garden room.

The project was a challenge for the architect because of the considerable size of the new addition. The delicate trellises helped visually reduce the volume of the windows by filling the open glass of the sliding doors with interesting textures and shapes. On the exterior, a sloping, pagoda-like roof gave the addition the necessary quaintness and charm it needed to blend easily with the original house.

A medley of natural materials gives the new space the soft, textural feel of a rustic screen

▼ A floor-to-ceiling window, backed by a trellis outside, illuminates the hallway. This space was once the home's stoop; it now connects the old part of the house with the sunroom addition.

▲ Exposed timbers on the existing stone gatehouse inspired the architect to build with rustic pine trimmed with redwood trellis. The flagstone patio makes the backyard a place for entertaining, too.

▲ *When your walls are all made with glass sliding doors, the view is as big as all outdoors. Imagine how ordinary this room would be without those redwood trellises outside. That one small design element transports the style back to the past.*

porch. Pine boards wrap the walls; fir planking covers the floor and ceiling. Unpainted wicker furniture, which once belonged to the owner's grandmother, adds to the room's mellow tone.

Dark finishes also help minimize the room's size, but they don't detract from its sunny disposition. The three exterior walls use five full sets of sliding glass doors and screens—including one 12-foot-wide door set on the rear wall. To keep the room comfortable in cold weather, they installed only high-quality, double-paned sliding doors with tight seals around the running gear.

New Season for a Farmhouse

The owners of this 1907 Victorian farmhouse bought it with the confidence that they had taken on a similar project before. However, in the 10 years they've been renovating and expanding the old house, they've run across a few situations they didn't foresee.

For, who can be totally prepared to discover 27 dump-truck loads of brush, weeds, and rubbish that have to be hauled away? Or who knew the chimney that seemed marginal would prove less so and have to be rebuilt? Or who would have predicted digging around the foundation and unearthing a nest of copperhead snakes?

▲ *From this angle, the home looks much as it did originally. But all the windows have been removed, reconditioned, and refitted.*

◄ *To blend an addition into a home, match the siding and roofing, scale new windows to match old ones, and let the new roofline repeat the pitch of the old one.*

Central to the owners' plans was increasing living space by adding on a new great-room. Most ceilings are low throughout the original house, giving rooms the squat character usually found in dwellings of this vintage. But the ceiling of the new 26×20-foot great-room rises with the roofline, and beams have been left open to create a space with an uplifting feeling. Those touring older rooms first feel the home's snug embrace. But as they walk into the addition, a new attitude unfolds before their eyes.

Lightly washed and naturally finished wood planking was chosen for walls and floors to maintain the historic ambience. But the great-room's door treatment tips off visitors to the recent date of the addition. Although the design takes a cue from the home's architecture, all that glazing and the geometry of the casings and trim certainly weren't done at the turn of the century. Nor were the skylights that help illuminate the space.

The room is artfully composed for display with a continuous shelf wrapping the room at the eight-foot level. It's the perfect spot for rows of baskets, which add texture to the room. Furnishings also strike the right chord with an emphasis on handcrafted painted pine.

◄ Antique touches help a new addition echo the feeling of an old house. Here, used brick and a vintage mantel team with homespun accessories to take the new space back in time.

▲ This addition's exterior matches the roof pitch of the old house and has the fresh drama of a vaulted ceiling inside. Although the space is essentially modern, rustic beams and country furnishings link it to the original house.

A Fresh Outlook

An addition that adds drama and excitement to a floor plan doesn't necessarily require the building of an elaborate, expensive wing or a whole new room. This Minnesota lakeside home shows how an addition of only a few square feet can inspire radical improvements to a home.

As the floor plan (*below*) shows, the only structural change on the exterior was the slight bump-out of a wall between the kitchen and family room. This diagonal wall allowed the kitchen layout to flip-flop, the family room to expand, and glass doors and windows to replace outside walls. With work already disrupting this area of the house, this was also the best time to move the laundry into a more isolated spot away from the entry and create a mudroom with plenty of storage and light.

The new orientation of the room emphasizes the importance of a lake view. Anyone standing at the new island sink in the kitchen can take in a soothing vista, while also enjoying the feeling that they are more a part of things in the family room. Rearranging the rooms allows more storage and an easier flow of traffic.

The butler's pantry was redesigned to include a sink and a dishwasher while still making room for 15 feet of countertop. As many as 60 people have come for dinner and the kitchen has been able to easily accommodate their needs and the

◄ *On winter evenings, the fireplace becomes the focal point of the family room. The plan (below) shows how traffic flow was improved when a doorway to the kitchen was opened near the stairwell.*

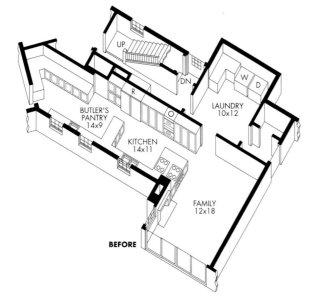

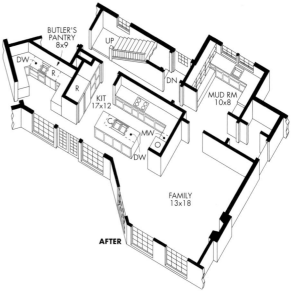

clean-up chores that followed. The design was completed with a refreshing balance of whites, sandy neutrals, wood tones, and a variety of natural textures—wood flooring, warm-toned kitchen cabinets, counters featuring peach-colored granite, and ceramic tiles at the backsplash and fireplace surround. Finally, thin planks were put up on the family room's fireplace wall and glazed to match the kitchen's cabinetry. It's a simple visual trick that strongly ties the two rooms together.

▲ *Floor-to-ceiling windows give those at the dining table an incredible lake view. Sunlight is also splashed on the table by a pair of skylights opening up the ceiling above.*

▲ *The view across the island's granite countertop is now open to the family room, so cooks won't feel isolated anymore. The cooking center includes double ovens, a microwave oven, and a warming drawer.*

DESIGN DETAIL

Overlooking an ingredient can ruin a supper, so don't miss these details when designing a kitchen:

■ Leave 18 to 24 inches of landing space on each side of a sink. There should be 15 inches to set items down near a refrigerator. And don't forget landing spots around microwave ovens and cooktops.

■ Allow space for the door swings of appliances. Will your refrigerator's door hit a cabinet? Will a dishwasher door block a passageway? Watch out for oven doors that push you back into other cabinets, too.

■ If you want an eating space in a smaller kitchen, consider making a counter an eating area that can double as a food-preparation center.

Building Up, Not Out

◄ *Instead of remaining an ordinary ranch, this house gained appeal with a second-floor addition. The dining room is located behind that five-window bay.*

Gaining extra space for a growing family poses a real challenge when you're living in a one-story ranch on a tight lot. With little room to spread out, the only way to grow is up.

The decision by the homeowners to add a second story was also prompted by the high quality of the California neighborhood in which this home is located. Although this home was modest, it could easily bear the cost of first-rate remodeling without a gain in resale value that would surpass the value of nearby homes.

Here's what was gained by the addition:

■ Upstairs, a new master bedroom suite and two bedrooms for the children were created.

■ Downstairs, the living room was transformed into a casual family room opening onto the kitchen. The dining room, which had been awkwardly pushed into a dark corner of the living room space, now nestles against a bank of windows and a patio. Whether dinner parties are formal or informal, the atmosphere is right.

■ A more efficient layout of main-floor rooms allows for better circulation, clearer separation of spaces, and the creation of a breakfast nook.

■ New terraces and landscaping in the front yard. Before renovations, the home's front facade lacked any originality. But it looks like an inviting villa today.

Brightening the house required more and larger windows. A tall bay made with five vertical windows was installed in the dining room bump-out, a large and strategically placed window topped with a rounded accent window was positioned above the stairwell to let in light while maintaining privacy, and corner windows were placed in an upstairs bedroom. Several skylights were also put in the addition's roof so upper rooms can grab sunshine and glimpses of stars.

Before beginning work, the homeowners realized the project would prove disruptive for neighbors—the same people they would be living next door to for years. So, they hosted what they called a demolition party. Neighbors were invited to view architectural plans, see the construction schedule, and get familiar with the work ahead of time, rather than springing it on them.

▲ *Detailing on the second floor includes the stairwell banister's cutout (above) and the balcony overlooking the living room (right).*

▼ *Rooms were tight before the second floor was added. Now the main floor's arrangement is relaxing.*

BEFORE

PATIO

BEDRM

DINING

LIVING

KITCHEN

ENTRY

BEDRM

BEDRM

AFTER

MASTER BEDRM

OPEN TO FAMILY

BEDRM

DN

BEDRM

UPPER LEVEL

AFTER

PATIO

BRKFST

BEDRM

FAMILY

KITCHEN

LDRY

UP

ENTRY

DINING

LIVING

PATIO

MAIN LEVEL

Warm-Welcome Entryways

Even before you answer the door, make sure your home's entry sends your visitors a warm greeting. The 1940s house (*right and below*) was a typical rambler—with little indication, architecturally, of where the front door was located. To make matters worse, the door opened right into the middle of the living room. An entryway addition easily solved both problems, pulling the entry forward to create a sunny vestibule with arched skylights and a tile floor. Transoms around the doorway add more light. A generous roof overhang now shields guests from the elements.

▲ *Wide brick columns give the entry a solid appearance. The door was surrounded by sidelight and transom windows with extra-thick frames to give the project more visual weight.*

◄ *Inside, the new entry is equally inviting, drawing guests toward the light above then into the rooms beyond. A tile floor impervious to tracked-in dirt relaxes guests and owners alike.*

▲ *The red brick steps leading up to the portico are the only hint of this Colonial Revival's original color. The half-thick columns, called pilasters, are attached to the wall on either side of the door.*

As with the 1940s house, the home shown *above* lacked an entry. Typical among many Colonial Revival-style homes, the front was barefaced, lacking any outside entry structure. Such blunt presentation may have been necessary in colonial Boston where the fronts of houses extended right up to the roadway with no projections to get in the way of passing carriages. Today, however, an entry portico adorned with stout classical columns is the better idea. Not only does this small addition offer big visual impact and increased curb appeal, but it also puts a protective roof over the heads of waiting guests.

Before adding an entry, explore your home's architectural heritage so your project can be just as sensitive to the past as this one. This will make the addition more pleasing aesthetically, and it will increase, rather than decrease, the value of your home. This entryway, for example, was added only after careful study of the home's roots in Federal architecture. Detailing such as the classical columns, the fan transom, and the brick walkway are all appropriate to the style. Inside, refinished floors, upgraded lighting, and repainted walls add to the new look.

To further enhance the makeover project, the entire front of the house was given a refreshing coat of soft gray paint. Contrasting white paint highlights the new porch detailing and under-the-eaves dentil molding.

Brave New Spaces

▲ *The addition extended the house out into the backyard and upward with a second story. All you see in this view was added to the house.*

▲ *The kitchen has all-new cabinetry and appliances. It takes inspiration from the past, but it will remain contemporary in its efficiency for years to come.*

The original layout of this home may sound familiar to many readers: The kitchen was a narrow, cramped galley; rooms that would otherwise offer wonderful views lacked enough windows, and the master bedroom suite was neither masterful nor sweet. The solution was to add outward and upward.

The project began on a sheet of graph paper. The homeowners needed space for a special table and they thought a modest kitchen bump-out would do the trick. One idea led to another, and soon they were reconfiguring the whole house. An architect helped them flesh out the details:

■ An expanded kitchen with a comfortable breakfast room. The breakfast nook offers views of the couple's parklike backyard and was, in fact, the space that inspired the entire project.

■ A warm sunroom addition. Its floor is made with ceramic paver tiles that give the space texture and color.

■ A new master suite in the second-story section of the addition. The new room features a closet almost as big as the couple's former bedroom. In the bathroom, there's a whirlpool tub and a steam shower.

As with most renovations, there were unexpected challenges along the way. Though it was originally believed that the existing roof would be adequate, it turned out the family had to replace it.

They also watched the budget climb far beyond their initial projections—a common occurrence when adding on. They found themselves agreeing to details, such as an elaborate oak hearth in the new den, for which they hadn't originally budgeted. When they took the time to write out these alterations as change orders, the project wrapped up smoothly. But when there was no written order, they faced difficult negotiations later.

▲ The den has been fashioned into an end-of-the-day retreat. For warmth, there's a natural gas fireplace and for entertainment, there's electronic gear.

▲ The wall of the sunroom looking out at the parklike backyard is filled with energy-efficient, double-paned windows that also muffle sound.

▶ The floor plan shows how the house more than doubled in size. It proves that a humble house can grow up to be a manse of some substance.

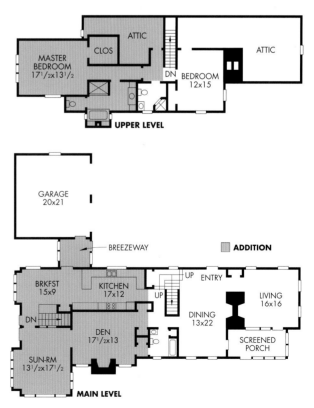

ATTIC

MASTER BEDROOM
17¹/₂x13¹/₂

CLOS

DN

BEDROOM
12x15

ATTIC

UPPER LEVEL

GARAGE
20x21

BREEZEWAY

■ **ADDITION**

BRKFST
15x9

KITCHEN
17x12

UP

ENTRY

UP

DN

DEN
17¹/₂x13

DINING
13x22

LIVING
16x16

SUN-RM
13¹/₂x17¹/₂

SCREENED PORCH

MAIN LEVEL

APPENDIX

For assistance in finding architects, remodeling contractors, designers, and information that can help you to successfully complete an addition project, these national organizations are valuable resources. None will tell you whom to hire, but they all offer insight into the selection process and will refer you to local or state chapters that can help.

For information about architects:
American Institute of Architecture
1735 New York Ave., NW
Washington, DC 20006
202/626-7300

For information about kitchen remodeling, Certified Kitchen Designers, and the latest kitchen design standards:
National Kitchen and Bath Association
687 Willow Grove St.
Hackettstown, NJ 07840
908/852-0033

For information about remodeling:
National Association of the Remodeling Industry
4301 N. Fairfax Dr., Suite 310
Arlington, VA 22203
800/966-7601

National Association of Home Builders
    Remodelers Council
1201 15th St., NW
Washington, DC 20005
800/368-5242

For information about the special problems with remodeling historic houses:
The National Trust for Historic Preservation
1785 Massachusetts Ave., NW
Washington, DC 20036
202/588-6000

For information about interior designers:
American Society of Interior Designers
608 Massachusetts Ave., NE
Washington, DC 20002
202/546-3480

For information about the Uniform Building Code:
International Conference of Building Officials
5360 S. Workman Mill Rd.
Whittier, CA 90601
310/699-0541
Note: The Uniform Building Code is used by more jurisdictions than any of the other building codes currently in force. Check with local government to see what code applies in the area where you live. Copies of that code are usually available through the agency or at bookstores.

Index

Numbers in bold indicate pages with photographs.

U.S. Units to Metric Equivalents		
To convert from	Multiply by	To get
Inches	25.4	Millimetres (mm)
Inches	2.54	Centimetres (cm)
Feet	30.48	Centimetres (cm)
Feet	0.3048	Metres (m)
Cubic Feet	28.316	Litres (l)

Metric Units to U.S. Equivalents		
To convert from	Multiply by	To get
Millimetres	0.0394	Inches
Centimetres	0.3937	Inches
Centimetres	0.0328	Feet
Metres	3.2808	Feet
Litres	0.0353	Cubic Feet

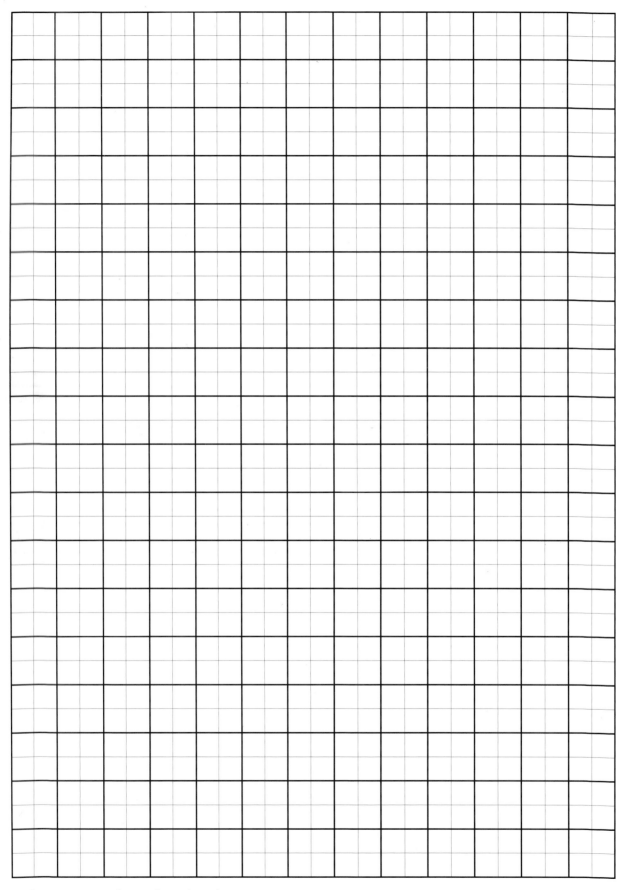

Light squares = 1 foot at ¼-inch scale
Bold squares = 1 foot at ½-inch scale